UNDERSTANDING INDIAN MUSIC

UNDERSTANDING INDIAN MUSIC

BABURAO JOSHI

GREENWOOD PRESS, PUBLISHERS
WESTPORT, CONNECTICUT

Library of Congress Cataloging in Publication Data

Joshi, Baburao.
    Understanding Indian music.

    Reprint of the 1963 ed. published by Asia Publ.
House, Bombay, New York.
    1. Music--India--History and criticism. I. Title.
ML338.J68 1974   781.7'54   73-15055 3 · 1 7 · 7 6
ISBN 0-8371-7156-3

Originally published in 1963 by Asia Publishing House,
Bombay, New York

Reprinted with the permission of Asia Publishing House, Inc.

Reprinted from an original copy in the collections of the
University of Illinois Library

First Greenwood Reprinting 1974
Second Greenwood Reprinting 1975

Library of Congress Catalog Card Number 73-15055

ISBN 0-8371-7156-3

Printed in the United States of America

CONTENTS

FOREWORD

EVERY student and lover of music will find *Understanding Indian Music* a very interesting discourse on Hindusthani Sangeet. The author Shri N. V. (alias Baburao) Joshi, the well-known Listener of music and musicologist of Kolhapur has, in these pages, dealt with music from the listener's point of view, lay as well as learned.

Music is relative in all its aspects. One is reminded of the famous saying of Lord Shree Krishna :

ये यथा मां प्रपद्यन्ते तांस्तथैव भजाम्यहम् ।

Ye Yatha Mam Prapadyante, Tans Tathaiva Bhajamyaham.

> They think of me in the form they love and even so
> do I manifest myself unto them

In describing the music as he " sees " it — and Baburao Joshi is a perfect observer — the author has discussed important and useful topics of Hindusthani music. His observations on them will go a long way in guiding the listeners, Indians as well as non-Indians, towards a correct appreciation of this great art, the national heritage of the Indian people.

This book will be a valuable addition to the libraries of all institutions of musical training and cultural centres.

Let me congratulate the author and wish him all success.

S. N. RATANJANKAR

PREFACE

ALL of us like music of one kind or other. But music, which conforms to true art, is not appreciated fully by all of us. No art can be enjoyed fully unless some sort of effort to grasp its basic principles and its technique is made. This is more so as regards Indian music which has a very complicated and subtle science of its own. The royal road to acquaint ourselves with this is, of course, to learn music itself. But very few of us have the capacity or opportunity to learn it. The lot of the majority of people is such that they are either totally uninitiated in or very slightly acquainted with the musical art. This book makes an humble attempt to initiate such people, who are not going to learn like students but simply listen. From actual experiments made in that direction, I am convinced that it is possible to kindle the interest of the average listener for classical music and to cultivate his taste for it, if his ears are properly trained with the help of suitable demonstrations. Written, therefore, with the main object of educating the lay listener to help him to appreciate Indian music, the book needs no apology.

Keeping this in mind, I have not entered into the intricacies of musical science or into the details of actual rendering of musical art. For the convenience of those who are not at all conversant with Indian music, I have taken special care to deal with some topics more elaborately and in a style that may suit such readers. Even so, the students of music and the music teachers would find this book useful from many other points. Along with basic facts, this book attempts to deal with the basic principles and *values* in music and with the ultimate ideology of the science and art of music. This would, I believe, help to give a proper perspective with which music should be studied or taught.

I am conscious that the musicians and the musicologists may not agree with some of my views or conclusions especially where they run counter to what is stated in old texts or what is traditionally being accepted. There is an impact in our music both from within and from without. The young generation is swayed by music other than classical or Indian too. It is, therefore, high time that our traditional assumptions and conceptions about music are rationally and experimentally tested and new and effective methods of education are evolved. Whatever that may be, I humbly entreat the musical experts that such few controversial points need not prevent them from giving anxious consideration to the novel experiment in appreciation and understanding Indian music which this book mainly aims at.

Much discussion in the book has to be supplemented by suitable demonstrations without which values in music may not be fully brought home to the lay listener. The book gives many useful hints as to how such demonstrations may be given.

The idea underlying the present book first appeared in my book *Sangeetache Rasagrahan* written in Marathi and published in 1956. But I was prompted to write this book at the suggestion of Lieut. General S. P. P. Thorat and Shri J. P. Naik who took keen interest in my experiment and also helped me in many ways for which I have to express my sense of gratitude.

I cannot close without acknowledging, with grateful thanks, the information I derived from the various books (mentioned in the Bibliography) and the assistance I got from various persons. First of all, I must make a special mention of Prof. G. R. Kokil of Kolhapur who gave me a thorough assistance while preparing the script. Rev. Father Robert Jacob, S. J., took the trouble of revising the whole script critically and making useful suggestions. Prof. A. Lobo of Bombay supplied me very useful information. My friend Shri J. L. Ranade also assisted me in various ways. Lastly, my sincere thanks are due to the Asia Publishing House for their prompt acceptance of my work and for neatly bringing out this book.

Padma Bhushan Dr. Ratanjankar, the veteran musicologist, has really obliged me by giving blessings to this book through his Foreword.

14-1-1963   BABURAO JOSHI
Kolhapur
Maharashtra, India

UNDERSTANDING INDIAN MUSIC

1. NEED FOR EDUCATION

Universality of Musical Appeal

OF ALL fine arts, music is the most intimate and fullest expression of human nature. Sound and rhythm, the two constituents of music instinctively attract almost everybody. We notice that the attention of a newly-born babe can easily be attracted to a stray sound. Since childhood the urge to produce a sound is displayed and musical tunes are imitated with ease. The native sense of rhythm is also there right from the beginning. The human body itself by its respiration, the beats of the pulse, the gait and the like displays that sense. No wonder, therefore, that the music produced by the harmonious blending of a variety of notes and rhythm should have an attraction for all.

Another reason for this universal attraction is that the pleasure derived from music is both from within and from without. One is not pleased only when one listens to others' music, but one can very well amuse oneself by one's own. For that, one need not be endowed with any musical faculty or even the gift of a voice. No accompaniment, nor any listener is necessary — nay, it is better if there is none. But I am quite sure that, in spite of all such handicaps, when left to oneself one does produce some tunes — even humming or whistling — enough to please oneself. The pleasure of listening to one's own voice is unique ; and, I think, that is the most natural manner of enjoyment for the human being. Moreover, if music is understood to mean, in a wider sense, whatever is sung or played in some form of rhythm, then music pervades every stratum of society. There is music in a beggar, a king, a rustic, a connoisseur, a pandit and a man of the jungle. And if one is not going to bother about the sort of music that is cherished — whether classical, light, folk, stage, film or any crooning or variety referred to as ' musical '— then *everyone* likes music.

The Science and Art of Music

If music has such a vast and popular sway, the propriety of a book, like the present, dealing with ' appreciation of music ' may very well be questioned. It may also be asked : ' Why then do we come across many people who say that they do not understand or appreciate music or even like it ? ' First of all we must admit that there is a considerable difference between simply ' liking ' a thing and ' understanding ' it. Appreciation is, so to say, liking with a sort of understanding or consciousness behind it. That is why, all people do cherish music of one kind or the other ; but all kinds of music are not cherished by everyone. Further, we must try to understand the distinction between ' music ', the ' science of music ' and the ' art of music '.   All music is not scientific music ; nor is all scientific music artistic. Let us take a few analogies. Everyone speaks some sort of language. But all spoken language does not amount to even an elegant conversation much less to an oration. All the images prepared by a potter or a craftsman do not pass for works of art, nor can all the numerous rhymed couplets be classified as classical poetry. In order to rise to the level of art, therefore, a musical work has to undergo many operations (*Sanskara*) and process of selection with reference to certain standards, discipline and prescriptions within the ambit of that art. So when people complain that they do not understand or do not like music, it is mostly with reference to the scientific and artistic aspects of music. For, in ordinary popular hits like ' Man Dole Mera Tan Dole ' or ' Tumsa Nahin Dekha ' there is nothing which a common man may dislike or need any understanding about. But as regards the understanding and appreciation of the scientific and artistic aspects of music, the common man experiences many a difficulty. In the following pages an attempt is made mainly to tackle that problem.

Given this important difference between music, the science of music and the art of music, it follows that all cannot derive pleasure by relishing the science and the art of music. For an understanding of this, it is necessary to know where one sphere ends and the other begins. The nature of the scientific structure and its underlying principles must broadly be understood. Further, one must have an idea as to what makes a scientific piece an artistic one and by what tests and standards the same can be judged. In other words, to understand such distinctions and niceties one must be either naturally endowed with a certain degree of ability or one must get oneself initiated into it. The task may be easy for some, while it may be a bit difficult for others. But none the less, it is idle to expect the ability to enjoy and appreciate a piece of art without any such capacity. You cannot enjoy a game of cricket or tennis unless you are conversant with the technique, niceties and the principles of the game. One who is not at all familiar with such a game will, not only, not find any interest in it ; but, on the contrary, he would perhaps consider the people watching the game for hours together under the scorching sun or in shivering cold as idiots or idlers. Needless to say, what holds good in the matter of everyday sport would apply in a much higher degree in the realm of an art like music.

Some Objections

But the proposition is not, however, readily accepted by all. They say that if pure joy and the vision of beauty are the invariable or necessary fruits of all classical music, then an uninitiated listener also must be able to share them. His enjoyment should not be, in any event, the less on account of his ignorance of the technique and the precepts of the musical art. If, on the contrary, such an effect is not produced in the listener and his interest fails, well, the defect must needs be with the art evidently. Why, then, is anyone at all called upon to engage in its study?

The argument is plausible enough and cannot be refuted easily. To awake an emotion and to enable the listener to have a glimpse into the world of beauty is certainly the function of music which is classical. And furthermore, what is genuinely beautiful and enchanting needs no telling that it is so. The charm of a rose flower or the fascinating beauty and coolness of moon-light under the cloudless canopy of the heavens would not be less charming because there is no one to describe it in vivid detail. Why, then, should we need any preparatory training for musical appreciation?

A little more reflection will, however, make it clear that this line of argument is based upon two wrong premises. It is a mistake to assume that any and every listener of a musical piece comprehends all its beauty and therefore is equally stirred by it emotionally. The way to any artistic goal may be through emotion ; but by itself emotion does not enable one to get a glimpse of artistic reality. The full appeal of art is not only through emotion ; the intellectual faculty also has to play its part. Even emotion needs to be refined before it can assimilate the content of art. However high the intensity of the transmitter may be, it would fail to produce the desired effect if the receptive capacity of your radio set is, for some reason, defective. The rich panorama of Nature is all around us, but are we not ordinarily ' blind ' to its beauty until some artist or poet draws our attention to it and makes us share his pleasure? Mere knowledge of reading and writing is not by itself an adequate equipment for appreciating fully a classical literary piece. If this were possible for us, numerous volumes of criticism upon the works of Shakespeare, Kalidas and others would have been a sheer waste. One may have an instinct or an aptitude ; but to have merely an aptitude or instinctive appreciation is not enough. In every art, therefore, the study, at least an understanding of its technique and discipline, is bound to find a large place. Music being the most imaginative and abstract of all arts, the importance of the study or understanding of the discipline cannot be gainsaid.[1]

All that Glitters . . .

Another fallacy lies in assuming that anything that is pleasing to the ear must needs be aesthetically appropriate. A visit to a picture gallery is enough to convince us that the pictures which readily engage our attention do not all stand the test of genuine art. Our early conceptions of what is beautiful and enjoyable do undergo

---

[1] It would be very interesting and instructive to note what Dr. C. Whitaker Wilson, the famous organist and pianist says in his book *How to Enjoy Music* published contemporaneously with the first publication of this book in Marathi. Though his remarks are with reference to Western music, they hold good as regards the problem under consideration:

' I have nothing to say about crooning, brass-band music or the types of stage production we now refer to as " musicals ". I think you must have already found out anything you want to know about them, even if you have not, I am quite unable to help you.

' Serious music is another matter. The art itself is so vast, and much of it is so complicated that unless you make some sort of effort to grip its principles and understand its oddities you lose on all counts. That would be a pity because you are going to miss so much enjoyment. Nothing can alter the fact that your enjoyment of music is proportionate to your depth of understanding. The more familiar you are with the way the musicians think the more you enjoy the result of their thinking.'

a change when we come of age. There is usually a time in our lives when Aesop's fables, cheap and smutty stories, detective thrillers and the like have their sway. It is only after the mind is mature that we come to discover their limited appeal and prepare ourselves to delve deep into what is genuine classical literature.

The cheap kind of music has a way of its own to fascinate the listener. Its composers take special care to make it attractive ' at first sight '. It is like processing and spicing foodstuff of low quality to make it savoury. The pleasure that is derived by a layman from many musical pieces is not due always to their intrinsic musical quality, but often depends upon other factors which are superfluous and unconnected with the art. Many film-songs have come to stay on account of the arresting appearance of the ' star ' or of the ravishing accompanying dances, or of the exceptionally fascinating voice of the play-back singer. Songs which have a sexy or sensuous appeal fascinate most of the listeners. We also come across a class of listeners who have a strong bias for female singers. Thus it is that certain inept and irrelevant factors come to stifle the musical quality and bring an unusually low standard of appreciation to bear upon the art. To treat all that glitters as gold, or everything that is huge as great and everything that attracts as beautiful is to mistake the sham for the real and to deny the delight that is due to what is genuine.

Training of the Ear

The task of musical appreciation, however, is not a very difficult one. It is true that the art of music is vast, its science is very intricate and to get proficiency in singing or playing on an instrument is by no means an easy achievement. But even so, one need not be deterred by these considerations. Those difficulties may confront persons who have actually to sing or play, but not persons who have simply to listen. The listener's ' eyes ' are trained and can distinguish easily between animate beings and inanimate objects, between various shades of colours and between what is beautiful and what is ugly. So also the listener's ' tongue ' is trained to distinguish between a variety of tastes. There is no reason why his ' ears ' should lag behind. The real point is that like the ' eyes ' and the ' tongue ', the ' ears ' must also be trained. They must be made 'attentive' to various notes, their combinations and to various shades of melodies the resulting pleasures of which were hitherto lost on them or against which they had shut themselves. My humble attempt in the succeeding pages would be, therefore, to show the listener the way to do it.

Hallmark of Indian Culture

Whether the task of appreciation is simple or otherwise, I think that everyone who is proud of Indian culture must acquaint himself with at least the basic structure of our music. For, our music can be described with pride as the very hallmark of Indian culture. Comparisons are, I know, odious; but I may be permitted to say that our system of music has so many unique and distinctive features to which no other system of music in the world can lay claim. The heritage of the *Raga* system, into which the developing musical culture found its expression from time to time, has no other parallel. No other *Tala* system has the reach of the intricate and very much developed science of *Tala* in Indian music. The importance given to the human voice, the use of the subtle microtones (*Shrutis*), the rich variety of ornamentations, the elaboration and improvisation and the freedom which the artist enjoys are some additional and distinctive features of our music.

2. VOICE-CULTURE AND EMBELLI

Limitations of the Book

BEFORE I proceed to deal with the subject proper, I should say something about the limited scope of this book. First of all, what I am going to say here, would entirely be with reference to the Northern Hindustani system of music and not the South Indian or Karnataka system of music. Though the main structure and the basic principles of both the systems are the same, they materially differ in many details including the method and manner of presentation also.

Likewise, I shall be using the terminology of Indian music and not that of Western music. The two systems so radically differ that it is difficult to find appropriate corresponding technical terms of one system to describe those of the other. As regards technical terms, I may further add that they would be employed only when absolutely necessary; and, that too, in their popular and current sense, and not strictly in their technical sense as given in the old musical treatises. It is not my intention to enter into the historical background and growth of music or into the intricacies and controversial points of the science of music. Such information is unnecessary and may, perhaps, confuse rather than benefit the listener. This book, let me repeat, is not meant for giving direct lessons in music to students who want to learn it. Its aim is modest — only to enable the listener to appreciate it. The royal road to do this is, no doubt, to learn music itself. But how many people have the capacity or the opportunity to learn music? And how many of them do actually learn it or are able to progress beyond, at the most, an advanced primary stage? This book, thus, is intended mainly for that vast majority of people who are totally uninitiated or only slightly acquainted with music. The musicians and musicologists need not suppose that the book will have no value from their point of view. They also would surely find here something interesting and educative too. At any rate, I hope that this book would serve show them what the layman's needs and expectations are about music — a point with which they also should be vitally concerned.

The word *Sangeet* (music) according to the *Shastras* includes three categories : (1) vocal music, (2) instrumental music, and (3) dancing. But popularly understood, *Sangeet* does not include dancing. Dancing differs from music both in form and the medium of expression. It has an independent science of its own. Hence I do not deal with that branch of art in this book. Of the remaining two, I would mostly concern myself with vocal music: for it is vocal music which has a primary importance in our system of music. Instrumental music is mostly an imitation of vocal music and needs no separate treatment in detail.

Basic Facts

It is necessary that readers should have some primary but important technical information about music. Many of the readers may be already having this information. It is, however, better to give it here in some detail for the convenience of all.

Music is based on seven primary *Swaras* (notes). Of these, two, the *Shadja* (the tonic) and the *Panchama* (the fifth) are fixed notes, in the sense that they have no variations (as flat and sharp) as the rest of the five notes have. Each of the four notes Ri, Ga, Dha and Ni, has a *Komal* variation which is lower in pitch than the original note. The remaining note Ma has, however, a *Tiwra* (sharp) variety. This makes a total of twelve notes in an octave (*Saptaka*). Table below shows the notes, their names, varieties, order and notation :

Serial No.	Name of the note	Abbreviation and Notation	Variety
1	Shadja	Sa	Fixed note
2	Rishabha	*Ri*	*Komal*
3	—	Ri	Shuddha
4	Gandhara	*Ga*	Komal
5	—	Ga	Shuddha
6	Madhyama	Ma	Shuddha
7	—	Mâ	Tiwra
8	Panchama	Pa	Fixed
9	Dhaiwata	*Dha*	Komal
10	—	Dha	Shuddha
11	Nishada	*Ni*	Komal
12	—	Ni	Shuddha

Notes in higher octave are shown by dots above (as G), those in lower octave are shown by dots below (as G̣a) while no dots are shown for those of the middle octave.

It should be noted that the first variations of Ri, Ga, Ma, Dha and Ni are all *Komal*; while the second are *Shuddha*. Some call these *Shuddha* varieties by the name *Tiwra*. The *Komal* variations are shown in italics. In case of Ma, however, there is a different nomenclature and different method of notation. The first variety of Ma is termed *Shuddha* and is shown without any sign ; while the second variety is termed *Tiwra* and is shown by a line above it (as Mâ) in the notation. The *Shuddha* variety of Ma is also called *Komal* by some.

As we ascend from Sa to Ni the pitch becomes higher and higher and this ascending succession of notes is called *Aroha*. In the reverse order, i.e., descending from Ni to Sa, the pitch becomes lower and lower and this descending succession of notes is called *Awaroha*. Each note has some fixed relation to the basic note or tonic, Sa. The reader may be spared all these mathematical relations ; but the peculiarity of some of them may usefully be noted. When we ascend from Sa to Ni, the next succeeding note after Ni is again Sa. Similarly all further notes repeat themselves in succession. So also, when we descend from the basic note Sa, the next note downwards is Ni and similarly all other notes are repeated in a descending order. These octaves or *Saptakas* are styled as (1) middle, the *Madhya*, (2) higher, the *Tara*, and (3) lower, the *Mandra*. Now the pitch of any note in *Tara Saptaka* is exactly the double of its identical note, i.e., its octave in the *Madhya Saptaka* and the pitch of any note in *Mandra Saptaka* is half of its octave in the *Madhya Saptaka*. Though the pitch differs, the sound of one note in one *Saptaka* and its octave in the other *Saptaka* is quite identical. There exists perfect unison in them so that they produce *absolute* consonance. Next in importance are the relations of *Shuddha* Ma and Pa with Sa. The ratios of Sa to Pa and Sa to Ma are 2: 3 and 3 : 4 respectively; while the ratios of Ma and Pa to upper Sa are also 2 : 3 and 3 : 4 respectively. The same would be evident from the following table of vibrations of the seven main notes :

First tetrachord	Sa	Ri	Ga	Ma
No. of vibrations	240	270	300	320
Second tetrachord	Pa	Dha	Ni	Sa
No. of vibrations	360	405	450	480

It is discovered that the Sa-Pa and Sa-Ma ratios give *perfect* consonance though not *absolute* consonance as in the case of a note and its parallel in upper or lower octave. These relations which are called the *Shadja-Panchama* and *Shadja-Madhyama Bhava* respectively have great importance in the musical system from another point of view also. A glance at the above table would reveal that each of the four notes of the first tetrachord bear the relation of *Shadja-Panchama* serially with each of the notes of the second tetrachord. Conversely, each note in the second tetrachord bears a Sa-Ma relation with each in the first. This would establish that the seven main notes are not arbitrarily chosen, but bear a relation with some other which is consonant.

Education by Demonstration

I know that mere reading of the information given hitherto would neither interest the average reader nor carry any conviction to him. The discussion must be aptly illustrated and explained. What is really important from the reader's point of view is not the memorizing of any technical terms or information, but the memorizing of the concrete exhibitions of them. For this, actual demonstrations are absolutely necessary. I expect that whatever I say here will be aptly illustrated and explained by a music-teacher by actual exhibitions of singing or playing on an instrument. As music expresses itself only through the medium of sound, the aid of such medium cannot be dispensed with while explaining any musical topic or problem. Scores of pages of description of a flower would not be as eloquent and effective as the actual exhibition of the flower itself. I am afraid that without such demonstrations much of my discussion would not be easily understood and many a conclusion of mine would not carry conviction. With all modesty, I may be permitted to state that I have given demonstrative lectures and made various experiments; and the present book is the outcome of the experience gained therefrom. This book would also serve as a guide to those who want to try similar experiments.

For example, some of the points made above can be conveniently illustrated by the use of a harmonium.[1] The peculiarity of this

[1] The use of the harmonium should, however, be made only for a limited purpose. Besides its tempered scale, the instrument has many other drawbacks which make it unsuitable for Indian music. I am suggesting its use on

instrument is that once any key is chosen as the tonic or basic note, the key that is immediately adjacent to it is *Komal* Ri, the immediate next is *Shuddha* Ri, and in this way one would get a complete octave of twelve notes. Thereafter the same notes again repeat. The artist chooses a note convenient to his or her voice. It is to be noted that between a man and a woman, a woman would choose necessarily a higher note (the interval being about four to five notes) as by nature the pitch of her voice is higher than that of a man. Generally speaking the male singers choose as their basic note one of the notes in the first tetrachord, that is Sa to Ma (C to F); while the women singers choose one in the second tetrachord, that is Pa to Sa (G to C).

Voice-culture

As sound is the only medium of expression for music, we must be very particular about the kind and quality of the sound we use. The sound in music can well be compared to the fabric of cloth. The kind and quality of cloth is necessarily determined by the fibre that is used. If the fibre is woollen, the cloth is woollen; if it is of fine thread, a fine cloth is manufactured. So what primarily matters in music is the quality of the sound or voice; for no good results can be expected with an inferior medium or material. As singing plays a dominant role in our music, our artists and scientists devoted much of their attention to the formation of voice. The process of training the voice is called *Swarasadhana*, voice-culture. But I would concern myself here with the qualities and effects which such a trained voice produces instead of the actual process by which such training is given; for, our listeners need not know about the latter aspect, a matter in which students of music alone are interested.

Musical Sweetness

It does not require any skill to distinguish between a sound which is on the whole sweet and one which is not so. Everyone is endowed with such a natural discriminating faculty. It is just as easy as distinguishing broadly between the white and the black. But all

the ground of convenience only. A note on the merits and the demerits of the instrument will be found in Chapter 6 of this book.

white is not of the same variety, and every variety has not the same shade. Similarly in sweetness there are different kinds, and in each kind there are different grades. To recognize these fine distinctions, it necessarily requires a trained ear. In the case of the human voice the difficulty is felt much more; for, strictly speaking, the voice differs with every individual.

The conception of sweetness in the art of our music, is different from natural sweetness — the quality of voice known as timbre. For musical fitness, mere natural qualities of voice do not suffice. The voice has specially to be prepared by long and sustained practice; as raw hide has to undergo a tanning process to be fit as quality leather. After such operations, not only do the natural qualities of the voice get a polish or culture, but the voice acquires so many other qualities necessary to give it a musical fitness. The sweetness which such a trained or cultured voice produces is considered to be the musical sweetness. The importance of this training is so great that even he who is not endowed with the natural gift of voice, but whose voice is trained in this way fares very well in the field of music.

Our scientists have by long experience and experiments ideally fixed the proper interval or ratio of each note with reference to the basic note. When any note exactly coincides with the pitch of this ideal note, and the note possesses other necessary qualities, we may say that the note so produced is the musically sweet note. I am aware that any such description would not help the reader to recognize in a particular case whether the true pitch is attained or not. For the standard notes are not separately provided with which any such comparison can be made. In actual practice, it is the artist who fixes the correct pitch himself. To recognize whether the artist has correctly attained the right pitch or not is really a difficult job and only long experience would help the listener in the matter. But in the case of simple and obvious consonances like unison of voice with the drone and *Shadja-Madhyama* or *Shadja-Panchama*, i.e., the fourth or fifth relations, the detection of sweetness or deviation from it is not very difficult. Whatever that may be, it should be noted that to have a trained, sweet and melodious voice is rightly considered to be the most important ' value ' in music.

To be musically fit, the note must not only be melodious, but it must possess many more qualities and must be free from a number of defects. We shall now examine some of these qualities and defects.

Steadiness and Continuity (Aas)

The note must remain steady, i.e., must not fluctuate, flicker or crack. Its intensity also must remain constant. If it is otherwise, that necessarily mars its sweetness and beauty. It must also be a prolonged note. Long-drawn notes produce a deeper and more sustained effect than short notes. To speak metaphorically, the difference in quality between the two is just like that between long-staple and short-staple cotton. The long notes sung in low rhythm impress deeply and have a better staying effect. Not only must a note be steady and sustained but continuity of voice must be maintained while improvising, i.e., while rendering various notes the breath must be sustained, without any break, for a pretty long time as far as practicable. The resilience of notes so created necessarily results in sustained attention of the listener.

Volume (Kas)

Another important quality to be achieved is the intensity or volume (Kas) of the voice. By volume, not only is the audibility of the note increased, but its effect on the ear is also deepened, as the impact of an intensive voice is bound to be greater. These qualities of the note are quite essential for scientific music which has to create a deeper and serious effect on the listener. When the voice of master artists is described in popular words like 'weighty', 'broad', or 'powerful', what is meant thereby is nothing more than that their voice is endowed with Kas, i.e., with intensity or volume.

Rasa

Above all, the note must have Rasa, that is, capacity to delight or please. The concept of Swara is something more than what is conveyed ordinarily by the term note. Etymologically the word Swara means 'self-illuminating' or 'self-shining'. In other words, it can be said that the note must have 'life' in it so as to become Swara. It is this lively element in the Swara which gives you the delight (Ananda) — technically called the Rasa.

Through *Swarasadhana* many other qualities like making the voice soft or tender (but not weak), making it pointed, resilient, sonorous and elastic are cultivated. It would suffice, however, if attention is paid to the main qualities of voice referred to above and their salutary effects on musical production.

It would be noted that all these qualities are not used at all times, that is, in every piece and in every form of music. The different forms of music, as also the different effects in music, require the use of different qualities of voice — a point which may be dealt with further at a later stage.

Faultless Note

Just as a singer has to achieve certain qualities while training the voice, he has also to eschew certain defects. Our *Shastrakaras* are, surprisingly enough, more eloquent while condemning these defects than while advocating the cause of merits. Following are a few instances in point.

All extended notes necessarily end with one of the vowels, e.g., in an *Akara* (A as in art), or *Ekara* (E as in eat). The pronunciation of these vowels must not be changed or deformed in any way such as A (A as in again or A as in apt), Ai (as in eye), Aey, Hyi, Oy, etc. Needless to say that such deviations mar the beauty of the note. Utterance of meaningless, unwanted and irrelevant letters like Ba, Hay, Ha, etc., is also prohibited. The sound produced must be clear, free and full. It should not be nasal, throaty or husky; nor should it be produced by jerks or with closed teeth. The pronunciations of the words of the song must not be blurred but clear. At the same time it should not be harsh but soft. This is not only because the listener should know what is being sung but because the appeal of the music itself is greater when the words are quite audible and eloquent, for every note finds a body in the words in which it clothes itself. The *Shastrakaras* went further and laid down as to what should be the proper facial expression, the legitimate flourishes of hands and the right position of the body while giving a musical performance — all of which do add to its cultural value. Unfortunately these mandates are observed more in the breach even by master-artists.[2]

[2] The teacher is expected to give suitable illustrations and demonstrations so as to impress on the students the importance and effects of the various qualities

Alankara (*Embellishment*)

The Indian musicians have paid great attention to the subject of *Alankaras* (ornamentation), i.e., embellishments. They are patterns made out of various combinations of notes or are in the form of suffixes or affixes to the main notes. Thus they not only adorn or beautify but even enrich the whole piece of music. In short, they play the same role as figures of speech do in literature. Let us examine a few important varieties of *Alankaras*.

KHATKA AND MURKI

These are the most popular varieties of *Alankaras*. They are formed by combination of three or four notes taken in rapid succession in the space of one *matra* (the measure of time) and can be written down as Dha Pa Pa, Ni Ni Dha, Pa Dha Pa Pa, Ga Ma Pa Ma. The readers will discover that they are quite familiar with these varieties as they are abundantly used in popular hits of light music like ' Koyaliya mat kara pukar ', ' Maine lakho ke bol ', ' Muze na bulao '. The peculiarity of these ornaments is that they quickly captivate the minds of the listeners and have a sensuous appeal — qualities which account for their popularity. They are, therefore, purposely used in songs which are intended to create amorous, gay, or playful effects.

MEEND (GLIDE)

This *Alankara* may not be as popular as the above but is of vital importance from the point of view of musical art. In simple terms, *Meend* can be described as a mode of joining two notes by means of a graceful glide. In a string instrument this can be illustrated in two ways. One, when the finger is moved from one note to the other without lifting it from the string. The other, when the string is rapidly pulled sideways to produce a higher pitched note and then brought back to the original place. This process has twofold importance. This mode of reaching from one note to another is naturally

of voice. The illustrations should be so chosen as to bring out clearly the contrast between effects produced with a particular quality and those produced without it; for example, he should choose a song which utilizes long and continuous notes and contrast it with one which uses short and intermittent notes.

very artistic as it has the smoothness and grace of gliding or skating instead of the awkward jerks or jolts resulting from jumping. Another great advantage is that in such a process all the intermediate notes, even the *Shrutis* (the microtones) are slightly touched and this results in continuity (*Aas*) and fullness. These qualities make this *Alankara*, unlike the others, an indispensable one in musical production and is used by able artists both in scientific and light varieties of music. *Meend* which enriches music and gives an artistic shape to it must be regarded as the highest *Alankara* in music.[3]

GAMAK

Gamak according to *Shastras* is as an ornament, in general, produced by the combination of notes and has in its fold a number of varieties including *Khatka, Murki, Andolana, Kampit,* etc. That means, the definition is wide enough to include any ornament which notes can produce or resolve. Another author defines it in a restricted manner as a pleasant tremor of notes, and this definition comes nearer to the special restricted variety by which the *Gamak* is now popularly understood. It is formed by joining two notes which are repeated in rapid succession giving a graceful guttural jerk at both extremities. The repetition gives it a sort of parabolic shape and due to the jerks at both ends creates a *Gadgadit* sound (throbbing or sort of sobbing thrill). I know that all this description will not give the listeners any idea of the *Gamak* unless they have attentively heard it before. However, I may draw their attention to the sound created by the motor car, after the self-starter button is pressed but before the machine actually starts. The sound so created is no doubt metallic but it is sufficient to give an idea of a *Gadgadit* sound.

Gamak is the most weighty ornament and is equally difficult to render. Only the master-artist makes use of it. It is specially suitable for scientific music to create a serious and serene atmosphere. *Gamak* is not only an independent ornament but serves also as

[3] *Ghasit, Khench* (skating and the pull) are other species of *Meend.* Of course, there are subtle distinctions between the three varieties. But it would do if all are taken to be denoted by the common name *Meend.* The teacher should exhibit the importance of *Meend.* Especially, he should show how a similar variation without the aid of *Meend* becomes inartistic and flat.

a special style of rendering notes. Other light ornaments like *Khatka* and *Murki*, when rendered in *Gamak* style assume seriousness and can enter the province of serious music. *Tanas* rendered in *Gamak* style assume also similar serious form. *Gamak* style of singing puts greater strain on the lungs and it is only the master-artist who can ably exhibit this style of singing.[4]

KANA (GRACE NOTE)

Not very showy but none the less important are *Alankaras* formed by grace notes. This ornament is produced by a slight *Sparsha* (touch) to the neighbouring note, or by producing only a *Kana* (bit) of the note. It is, as it were, a suffix or a prefix to the main note. There are various ways of rendering the grace notes and they have their different technical names also. These grace notes both augment and adorn the main note and as such this type must be included in the essential group of *Alankaras*.[5]

TANA

No listener of Indian music can afford to be ignorant of that species of *Alankaras* called *Tana* which can be described as rapid succession of notes. Our singing, especially our scientific singing, is so full of *Tanas* that popularly the methodical singing is equated to *Tanabazi* (indulging in or predominance of *Tanas*). This remark is evoked sometimes as an appreciation and sometimes as a criticism too. Some listeners are so enamoured by the *Tana*-aspect of the singing that the more proficient the singer is in rendering

---

[4] The teacher should well prepare himself and exhibit the *Gamak* ornament. The following oft-repeated *Alapas* in *Darabari Kanada* Ri Ri Sa, *Ni* Sa, *Ni* Sa, Ri Ri Sa *Ni Dha*; or those in *Naiki Kanada* Ni *Ni* Pa, Ma Pa Ma Pa, *Ni Ni* Pa Ma, Pa *Ni Ni* Pa Ma *Ga*, are good illustrations where *Gamak* is required to be used. *Alapas* and *Tanas* in *Hindol* or *Marwa* would serve as instances to exhibit the *Gamak* style of singing.

[5] The following illustration would help the teacher. The bracketed note is the grace note and it is expected to be rendered by a quick touch only.
(Ma) *Ga*, (Ma) *Ga*, (Ma) *Ga*, Ma as in *Miya Malhar*.
Ma Ma Ma (Ma) Ri as in *Kedar*.
Sa (Ri) Sa, Pa (Dha) Pa,
(Ri *Ni*) Sa, (Dha Ma) Pa.
Ga (Pa Ri) Ga, as in *Shankara*.

M 2

the *Tanas*, and greater his indulgence in it, the higher he rises in their estimation, and greater is their interest in his performance. The effect on others, however, is otherwise. Their patience is worn out by the apparent monotony and the battery of *Tanas*, so that their interest not only flags in such a performance but they try to keep away from serious musical performances in general.

It is no surprise that *Tanas* should create such divergent effects. Really speaking, *Tanas* are but a species of *Alankaras*. In simple words they can be described as a rapid succession or variation of notes. Its quick rhythm, which serves as a relief or contrast to the slow motion *Alap Gayaki* is its first attraction. The display of dexterity of voice, the novelty in patterns and the spectacular effect created by these, further account for the attraction of *Tanas*. So, when *Tanas* are resorted to as the ' finishing strokes ' after a full-fledged *Alap Gayaki*, their importance and attraction in musical development cannot be in any way denied or diminished.[6]

But unfortunately our singing (even light varieties are no excep‐ tion) is overburdened with *Tanabazi*. The musicians who indulge in it and the audience which cherishes it both labour under a misconception of the proper proportion or relative importance of *Tanas* in the system of music. Singing or playing ought to have a predominance of *Alaps* which really build the structure of a *Raga* and which are responsible for all the appeal that music has.

The reasons for the excessive attraction for *Tanas* are not far to seek. It is easier to acquire proficiency in *Tanas* than in *Alaps*. Between the two, it is difficult for the average listener to grasp the implication and to understand the intricacies of *Alaps*. He is, there‐ fore, readily attracted towards *Tanas* which have a comparatively superficial and cheaper sort of appeal. It is high time that this indulgence in *Tanabazi* and the extravagant fascination for it is checked.

ALAP

As said above, the emphasis, in any musical production, must be given to *Alaps* instead of to any ornamentation or *Tanas*. *Alap*

---

[6] The teacher should illustrate different varieties of *Tanas* such as *Sapat-Tana, Gamak-Tana, Chakri-Tana, Bol-Tana,* etc. If possible, *Tanas* which rest on some prominent note for a while and again continue could also be demonstrated with advantage.

plays a very important role in musical production. The *Raga* is, first of all, revealed by the musical composition of the song. But music does not, and should not, end with mere reproduction of the already composed notes. The artist is expected to develop and expand the *Raga* theme. This is done through *Alaps*. The function of *Alaps* is, thus, primarily to unfold the *Raga* scheme. It helps the audience to enter into the ' spirit ' or ' mood ' of the *Raga* — technically called the *Rasa* of the *Raga*. To do this, no words are really necessary. The poetic theme has very little to do with the *Raga* theme. In classical music, at least, it is the contemplative part of the *Raga* and not the poetical content which the artist is expected to reveal. In that way, *Alap* is the pure and abstract music; so to say, ' a song without words ', and its role in musical production is unique.

Before closing this chapter, I have to say that whatever may be the importance of *Alankaras* in music, they should, like *Tanas*, be used with discrimination. Especially should the use of *Alankaras* which are merely ornaments and do not form the integral part of music be very restricted. In the case of real ornaments also, one cannot afford to be indiscreet. Decking the body with too many ornaments would, certainly, be looked upon as a sign of bad taste. In literature idiomatic phrases, metaphors, and similes do enrich the style; but their injudicious use tends to lower the standard of the literary piece. Similarly, the indiscreet use of *Alankaras* in music gives it a cheap tone. The artists should therefore, try to maintain the dignity and beauty of their style without the aid of ornamentation as far as possible. But such a course is difficult and the temptation to use *Alankaras* — which have also an immediate attraction for the uninitiated listener — increases. In the choice of *Alankaras* also, the right one, at the right place, must be made. Some *Alankaras*, as we have seen, are suitable for serious types of music, while others are suitable for lighter varieties. But, unfortunately, their places are interchanged resulting in a certain mongrel effect. All this goes on — or is tolerated — because the uninitiated listener is fascinated by the inordinate use of the *Alankaras*. My intention in entering into this elaborate discussion is, therefore, to draw the attention of the listener and the musician alike so that they may put a check on this misuse or overuse of *Alankaras*.

3. RAGA AND TALA

THE *Raga* system is the most unique and glorious feature of Indian music. Nay, it is the very backbone of our musical structure. No form of music, whether classical or light, can have existence without it. Even the simplest types of folk-music do follow the *Raga Tatwa* (the principle of *Raga*), though perhaps not the full scale of a *Raga*.

That simple types of folk-music should reveal *Raga Tatwa* would surprise many. The *Raga* system is, no doubt, the most complicated and scientifically evolved part of our music. It is no sudden and lucky invention. It is not that, on one fine morning, a few scientists made an invention of it or that a few artists sat together and brought about its creation. Like language, music was born; and like language its origin must be in the instinct of the masses themselves. But though natural in origin and simple in form, music did not remain static. Being the living embodiment of the inward urge of inspiration, like any other art, music also has the vital principle of growth. But the art of music was long in its growth; and was full of forces and influences from within and from without. Though originally the talented artists took their inspiration from the simple folk-song, their creative genius, their incessant hunt for finding something novel and beautiful and their powerful desire for self-expression gave rise to thousands of artistic patterns and hundreds of scales of music. The social, religious and cultural influences and the impact of different races brought about various forms of music and gave birth to innumerable songs depicting human life. The gradual discovery of string and rhythmical instruments added much to the richness and fullness of music. Side by side, the scientists kept themselves busy in discovering some law and order, i.e., the basic concept of *Raga*, prepared its grammar and tried to bring the art under the sway of a scientific order of an elaborate scheme, giving the art of music a science and discipline of *Raga*. But it was not in the artist's nature to remain always within the bounds of rigid science. He deviated from the rigid rules and gave birth to new and original combinations. The scientists, in their turn, found out

20

new scientific bases for such deviations also. This accounts for
the division of Indian music into two somewhat diverse systems
of the North and the South and the various schools of thought
in each system. In short, the highly developed *Raga* system of the
present day is the result of a very, very long process of evolution
from the simplest types of folk-music. It is interesting to note that
this was not merely a one-way traffic. As folk-music gave inspiration to the *Raga* system, the *Raga* system also influenced folk
music. Music being so essentially an art of human creation, it
cannot, whatever height it may reach, remain totally detached from
the mass-music. It is no wonder, therefore, that folk-music should
reveal the rudiments and glimpses of a system which has evolved
out of it.

What is a Raga?

Let us see what is meant by a *Raga*. In simple words *Raga* is a
melodic law or order. Technically, it is a melody type based on a
modal scale. We have already seen that in an octave, there are
seven main notes which can be divided into two tetrachords, i.e.,
from the basic note to the fourth note and from the fifth to the
upper tonic. Now in a *Raga* formation, the following main rules
are observed :

(1) At least five main notes must be employed.
(2) The *Shadja* is necessarily an indispensable note. So also
two notes, at least, from each tetrachord must be utilized.
(3) It must not exclude both *Madhyama* and *Panchama* notes.
(4) It should not use both flat and sharp varieties of the same
note consecutively.
(5) But the most important rule of the *Raga* system can be
found in one of its apt definitions : ' That which delights or charms
is *Raga* '. (*Ranjayati iti Raga.*) This means that a *Raga* scale must
have essentially aesthetic potentialities, or must be capable of
giving artistic experience. This important rule is responsible
for discarding hundreds of *Raga* scales which would have otherwise been mathematically possible even by observing the above
four rules.[1]

[1] The teacher should illustrate the above rules. He should take different
instances of *Ragas* which use equal number of notes both in ascent or descent

Another important feature of *Raga* is the use of *Vadi* and *Samvadi* notes. A note which is the most dominant in the *Raga* is called its *Vadi*. Next in importance to the *Vadi* note is the *Samvadi* — the complement of *Vadi* note. If *Vadi* is in one tetrachord, the *Samvadi* is necessarily in the other ; and they are so related that one bears the fourth or fifth note-relation to the other. These two notes and their relations to the tonic, mainly determine the character or the mood of the *Raga*.

In one sense, *Raga* determines ' the theme ' or ' the ground plan ' of the musical piece which the artist has to develop, at length or otherwise, according to his abilities. In another sense, *Raga* puts a restriction on the musical development. The mandate is that once an artist chooses to sing or play a song in a particular *Raga*, he has to adhere strictly to the notes permissible in that *Raga* and to its particular way of using any note in it. In other words, he is not to touch a note which is *Nishiddha* (prohibited) in that *Raga* (as *Ni* in *Bhoop*); nor to produce a note in a fashion not permissible (Ri in descent only and not in ascent as in *Bageshri*). The composition of the song as well as all *Alaps, Alankaras, Bol-Tanas, Tanas*, etc. in it must adhere to the rules of the *Raga*.[2]

I have already stated that though thousands of *Ragas* could have been formulated, yet only few stood the essential test of making an aesthetic appeal (*Ranjakatva*). The number of *Ragas* which have so survived is about two hundred — a number too big even for a great artist to have a working knowledge of all of them. In practice, it has been found that the range of *Ragas* known to an artist varies from about seventy-five to hundred only. Even here, the *Ragas* over which an artist has complete mastery and which he sings off and on, dwindles to a half. In short, the list of popular *Ragas* is in the vicinity of fifty only; and I may add further, that it would suffice for the average listener if he is able to recognize

(*Bhoop*); which use more notes in descent than in ascent (*Bhimpalas*); which take a note in a particular way (*Bihag*) and which employs even all twelve notes sometimes (*Bhairavi*). He should illustrate the importance of *Vadi* and *Samvadi* notes.

[2] Artists sometimes do touch even a *Nishiddha* note to heighten the effect of the *Raga*. But that is, after all, an exception and such licenses are taken by great artists only.

The cases of some particular *Ragas* and forms of music where deviations from strict rules are permissible stand on a different footing, to which reference will be made later on.

the most current and popular among them, say, about thirty only
— a list of which is given below.

To acquaint oneself with thirty *Ragas* is by no means an easy
job for a lay listener. His main difficulty is that he does not possess
the *Swaradnyana* (knowledge of *Swaras*) or the capacity to identify
a particular note — a quality which is very essential in order to
distinguish one scale from the other. The grouping of *Ragas* in
Thatas or *Melas* (modes or scales), or grouping them on the basis
of *Vadi* and *Samvadi* notes, would not help such a listener. For
these and such other methods of grouping, presuppose a definite
knowledge of different *Swaras* which an ordinary listener rarely has.

Classification of Ragas

For convenience, I have divided the list of desired *Ragas* into the
following three groups :

GROUP I

Light — Licentious

(1) *Bhairavi*, (2) *Pilu*, (3) *Kafi*, (4) *Tilakkamod*, (5) *Mand*, (6)
Khamaj, (7) *Jogi*, (8) *Pahadi*.

GROUP II

Scientific — Easy

(9) *Yaman*, (10) *Bhimpalas*, (11) *Bhoop*, (12) *Basant*, (13) *Durga*,
(14) *Bageshri*, (15) *Puriya*, (16) *Shankara*, (17) *Bihag*, (18) *Sarang*,
(19) *Bahar*, (20) *Tilang*.

GROUP III

Scientific — Serious

(21) *Malakounsa*, (22) *Todi*, (23) *Bhairav*, (24) *Jaunpuri*, (25) *Poorvi*,
(26) *Miyamalhar*, (27) *Jayjayvanti*, (28) *Kedar*, (29) *Adana* and
(30) *Bilawal*.

The first group comprises the most popular *Ragas*. These *Ragas*
are used in all forms of light varieties like *Thumri, Gazal, Bhava-
geet, Tappa* and others. So also all sorts of folk-music utilize,
though not the full, a part of a *Raga* out of this group. Another
important peculiarity of the *Ragas* of this group is that they are
of a ' loose character '. We have seen that a *Raga* must not use
prohibited notes, nor must it use notes in a prohibited manner.
But in the case of *Ragas* of this group, deviations from the strict
observance of these rules are permissible. So while developing a

light variety in the first group of *Ragas* not only is a prohibited
note touched, but even a group of notes or melodies which clearly
belongs to another different *Raga* is freely dwelt upon.[3] All this
is done, of course, very artistically and to heighten the emotional
appeal of the particular piece. We shall consider these playful
deviations in detail while dealing with forms of light music.

The second and third groups consist of *Ragas* which do follow
the strict rules and hence I have styled them as ' Scientific '. The
Ragas in the second group are comparatively easier to understand
and easier to render than those in the third and hence are more
popular too. The third is the more difficult group and the effect
of the *Ragas* of this group is more serious than those of the second.
I am aware that there are many more *Ragas* which can be included
also in the third group. The first two groups are illustrative, and
not exhaustive.

It may be quite a surprise to the Indian listener to know that he
is already familiar with more than a dozen of the *Ragas* enumerated
above. Since childhood he is listening to hundreds of songs
of various kinds. It is quite likely that he is even able to reproduce some of them, of course, in his own humble way. Still
many more he may very well be remembering. If this is so, he
cannot afford to be totally ignorant of some of the above *Ragas*.
His only deficiency must be that he may not be knowing the
names of the *Ragas* of the songs he is familiar with. But if he
succeeds in detecting the title of the *Ragas* I am sure he will be
pleased with the discovery.

Direct Method

But whether the listener knows anything of the *Ragas* or not, the
only method by which acquaintance of *Ragas* is possible, in the case
of an uninitiated listener, is the ' direct method ' of teaching a thing
by an actual demonstration of it. No other shorter or easier method
is either possible or desirable, because of the lack of *Swaradnyana*
to which I have already made a reference before. In the following
pages I am attempting to suggest certain ways of acquainting oneself with *Ragas* by the direct method.

[3] Following are some instances in point : *Tiwra Nishad* in *Kafi, Tiwra
Gandhara* in *Bhimpalas*, and all the twelve notes in *Bhairavi.* Mixing melodies
from *Sarang* and *Desh* in *Tilakkamod* and from *Patadeep* in *Kafi.*

Colour System

But before I do so, let me take the reader into the analogy of the system of colours. Every *Raga* has a mood of its own, or in other words, a colour of its own, which gives it an individualistic character. There are certain colours which are quite distinct from each other such as black, white, green, red, etc. There are some which are merely the shades of a particular colour (like blue, navy-blue, dark-blue and peacock-blue); or which are the mixtures of two. In the *Raga* system, too, there are certain *Ragas* the moods or features of which are too distinctive to be mistaken for one another (*Bhairava, Bhoop; Kafi, Todi*). Again there are certain *Ragas* which are but derivatives of the main parent *Raga* (like *Bihag, Bihagda; Bhairava, Ramkali; Todi, Gujari Todi*) and some are but mixtures of two *Ragas* (like *Poorva-Kalyan; Basant-Bahar*). So if the parent *Raga* is recognized or the component *Ragas* are recognized that would facilitate recognition of their derivatives or mixtures respectively. Even if the listener mistakes the parent for the derivative, it would not matter much. This way, by memorizing a few *Ragas*, a clue to the recognition of many more could be found.

This analogy would help to illustrate another point also. How do we recognize colours? Do we, as laymen, know anything about their source, elements, formation and manufacture? In spite of this ignorance of ours we know their names, can distinguish a large number of them and can enjoy their various shades too. The only way by which we are able to do this is the direct visual training our eyes had by their constant association. The same is possible in the case of *Ragas*, provided one pays a constant attention to it as ' audible images '. Therefore, what little one knows about musical melodies, one has to memorize them as norms and try to compare them with other melodies. One would soon develop a sense of finding identical or similar moods or colours in music.

The teacher is expected to illustrate a *Raga* by various methods. He should, first of all, select *Ragas* which are distinct from each other and sing a number of songs, differently composed, of the same *Raga*. As far as possible the songs should be familiar or popular with the particular audience before him. Then certain peculiarities of the *Raga* should be brought out. The predominance of the *Vadi* note in certain *Ragas* (Ri in *Jayjaywanti*, Dha in *Hamir*) the oft-repeated melodies in certain *Ragas* (Pa Má Ga Ma Ga in

Bihag; Ma Pa *Ga* Ri in *Kafi*), should be impressed on the listeners. For, these and others serve as ' identification marks ' of a *Raga*. He should sing some unfamiliar songs in familiar *Ragas*, or produce certain *Alaps* only and ask the listeners to recognize their *Ragas* — such a process would give them a stimulus.

Of course, all this presupposes a very active cooperation, — a student-like attitude — on the part of the listener, without which this most difficult art of musical appreciation would not be achieved.

It is my conviction, supported by experience, that this method is most effective to acquaint oneself with various *Ragas*. But, I would not be surprised if the listener is not successful in gaining good acquaintance with the *Ragas*. But in spite of this, I would insist on such an experiment. Even a failure in such an experiment would bring home to the listener the two main aspects of a *Raga*, namely, that every *Raga* has a mood of its own and that it has an individualistic character too. This revelation would necessarily deepen the interest of the listener and add to his pleasure, and I think this is, by no means, an ordinary achievement.

Before closing this important topic I shall briefly refer to two objections taken to the *Raga* system. The *Raga* has to conform to certain rules. It is asked whether there should be such restrictions in the sphere of art and whether these are hindrances in the way of artists. I think, to treat the *Raga*-rules as hindrances would be a mistake. We have seen that primarily *Ragas* came into existence first and the rules were later on framed on the basis of actual creation. The main idea underlying these rules is to assure an aesthetic potentiality and to give an individual characteristic to the *Raga*. Thus the rules help rather than obstruct musical production. Besides, as in life, so in the field of art there is no such thing as absolute freedom. Freedom is not mere licentiousness, to do anything, at any time and anywhere. The principle of aesthetic beauty in every art enjoins a discipline on the medium without which art cannot exist. So, every art has its own limitations of form and medium of expression. It has also to follow its own technique. Nay, the artist's skill and ability are really tested when within particular bounds he is able to explore all the possibilities. Whatever that may be, our experience shows that the various rules of the *Raga* system have never put any limitations on the elaborate exposition of art by the artist. On the contrary, they have enabled him to show off his utmost abilities and skill.

Another objection is as regards the monotonous effect of the *Raga*. The composition of the song, its development by means of *Alaps, Tanas,* etc. are but designs carved out of the same *Raga*. It is not surprising, therefore, that an uninitiated listener and especially a foreigner should feel that all this tends to reveal but one mood or depict one colour only. This feeling is confirmed by repetitions of the same designs by some of our artists. But if the charge is against the system, I have, forthwith to say, with due deference to the objectors, that this feeling is mainly due to the inability of the listener to distinguish between the subtleties and the shades of that particular mood and his inability to appreciate the niceties and the intricacies of its unfolding. To a distant and unmindful observer all leaves may appear alike but a closer study would disclose the thousands of distinctive shades and shapes amongst them. All words of an unknown language sound alike. But it would, certainly, be wrong to suppose that all of them have the same meaning. A closer study of music, or at least conscious and constant attention to it, would reveal that there are innumerable attractive and beautiful designs and that there are hundreds of shades in the scales, the realization of which would ultimately bring the listener much pleasure hitherto hidden.

Tala System

The idea of rhythm, *Laya*, is not only peculiar to music; but it is universal. The constant rotations of the planets, the cycles of time, the heart beats, the rotating machines — all exhibit the *Laya Tatwa* (the principle of rhythm). Our attraction for it, as observed before, is also natural. In music, rhythm plays a very vital role. It, first of all, regulates the movement of notes but for which music would be merely flourishes of notes in the wilderness. Secondly, it gives vitality to the musical piece. Otherwise, music without *Laya* would be as a body without bones. To take another simile, *Laya* is just like the cross thread (weft) which weaves through the lengthwise threads (warp) of notes.

In Indian music, *Laya* is exhibited through the *Tala* system. Like *Raga*, Indian musicians also evolved a very developed, elaborate and intricate science of *Tala*, which no other musical system of the world can equal. It plays two important roles in our music. Primarily, it serves as an accompaniment to vocal and instrumental music. Its secondary role is that of a solo-playing on *tabala* or *mridanga*, the two important instruments of *Tala*-accompaniment. This solo-playing has a very elaborate, intricate but equally interesting science of its own — rather too difficult for the average listener to get any insight into it. Why, even the singer finds it difficult to grasp it fully. The average listener would certainly derive pleasure from the overpowering effect which is brought about by the fullness of the sound of the instrument and by getting into the spirit of the *Laya*. Beyond this, I cannot help the listener more, as the subject cannot be dealt with exhaustively in the limited scope of this book.

Tala as an accompaniment stands on a somewhat simpler basis. Let us first understand the difference between *Laya* and *Tala* which are commonly misunderstood to be synonymous. *Laya* can be defined as the constant interval of time continuously maintained in repeated stress of any kind. *Laya* is thus a continuous movement in space of time. *Tala* puts a limit to it by dividing the time at a certain desired interval. The constant interval between two ticks of a second is its *Laya*, the minute which measures sixty seconds is the *Tala* (Time-cycle) while the second, the time-unit, is the *Matra* (Beat).

The pendulum would serve for another illustration. The constant interval of time required for the pendulum to oscillate from one end to the other, each time, is the *Laya* of the pendulum. The said interval taken once is a *Matra*, the time-unit. Now supposing that after completion of every four or six such oscillations the pendulum strikes a sound, then each four or six *Matras* would constitute a *Tala* of four or six *Matras* respectively. The first *Matra* giving a strike in each cycle is called the *Sama*, or the *Avasana* (arrival point) of the *Tala*. Thus *Tala* is a time-cycle made up of a certain number of *Matras*. Now the *Laya* of a pendulum can be made fast or slow by moving the position of the suspended bob upwards or downwards. So in music, the *Laya* can be varied in different tempos : *Vilambit* (slow), *Madhya* (medium) and *Druta* (fast). It should be noted that *Laya* may change while *Tala* remains constant; and *Tala* may change while *Laya* remains constant. The *Talas* differ mainly with the number of *Matras* allotted to them. Our artists have utilized, so far, no less than thirty-five such time-scales. In course of time, however, like *Ragas*, their number dwindled; so that now about fifteen *Talas* have remained in current practice. Following is the list of names of a few important ones. The figures in brackets show the corresponding number of *Matras* of the *Tala*.

GROUP I

Fast Tempo — Popular.
Kerwa (4); *Dhumali* (4); *Dadra* (6); *Teen Tala* (8);

GROUP II

Slow Tempo — Serious.
Deepchandi (7); *Zaptala* (10); *Ektala* (12); *Vilambit Teen Tala* (16); *Jhumra* (14).

The first group of *Talas* is played generally in fast tempo and they are more popular in the sense that most of the lighter varieties and all folk-music utilize these *Talas*. For serious music, the *Talas* in the second group which are generally slow in tempo, are used.

To understand the *tabla*-playing even in accompaniment, one has first to know about the peculiar *Bols* (alphabet of *Tala*) that are used for various *Talas*. One has to get acquainted with their ornamentation, improvisation, the bars used therein, the points of stress and such other details. The average listener would, therefore, face the same difficulty which he would in the case of *tabla*-solo-playing. I would not, therefore, trouble the listener with those details, but would make a few observations to enable him to have some insight into this difficult branch of music.

The difficulty in the appreciation of *tabla*-playing arises mainly on account of the tonal deficiency of the instruments utilized for it. Unlike all other musical instruments, the *Tala* instruments produce but one musical note, mostly the tonic to which the instrument is tuned. By means of fingers, pressure of the palm and other manipulations many more sounds are produced, but they are all non-musical. These non-musical sounds which can be called the language of *Tala*, are no doubt, quite distinct and have a separate significance of their own. They serve as a relief to the monotony created by the single note of the *tabla*. Why, the cooing, the whisper, the murmur and the resonance of the *Bayan* or *Dugga* (the left hand instrument) have a greater appeal than that of the musical sound of the *tabla*. But to understand all these subtle non-musical sounds is no less difficult than to understand the meaning of transmitting signals in telegraphy. Nothing short of a study of the alphabet and the science of the *Tala* system and its effects can help anyone.

Though not the *Tala*, the continuous flow of *Laya*, in a musical piece, can be easily understood. The attraction for *Laya*, as said before, is inherent in every individual. Of course, for appreciation of *Laya* in music, one has to cultivate that faculty a little more. Where, in the case of the first group of *Talas*, the *Laya* is faster and the *Matras* are smaller, the listener would find no difficulty to be one with the flow of the *Laya*. That is why these *Talas* are used in the case of all folk-music and other popular light varieties. But in *Talas* of slow tempo (as of the second group) the matter is not so easy and only after constant association and careful attention, the lay listener would get into the spirit of the *Vilambit* (slow) *Laya*.

The importance of *Sama* or *Avasana* (exhibited by a stroke or clap of hand also) which is the first beat of the *Tala* or the arrival point of the *Tala* should particularly be noted. All singing or playing must converge on or ' get to a *Sama* ' at various times and places. Specially, the important note in the ' burden of the song ' must coincide with *Sama* often and often. By so doing, the 'burden' is discharged so to say and the artist gets a little rest which prepares him to take a further flight.

The convergence of singing or playing to the *Sama* of the *Tala* which can be also described as ' catching of the *Sama* ' is a ' must ' in our musical performance. Failure to achieve the same would reflect very badly on the ability of the artist. Its artistic achievement, on the contrary, secures great applause from the audience. Nay, it is considered to be the duty of the audience to respond properly at such a juncture. So, if one wants to justify his place in such an audience, one must be conversant with this technique. This is easier in the case of the *Talas* of the first group, which repeat themselves at short intervals; but not so with the *Talas* of the second group of slow tempo.

The artist's proficiency does not end merely with the ' catching ' of the *Sama* properly. The whole performance must exhibit the sense of rhythm. The golden wire of *Laya* must be woven not only through the composition proper but also through all *Alaps*, *Tanas*, etc. It may not be patent every time, but the *Laya*-consciousness must be there, latent at least. The performance which reveals such a thorough consciousness is classed very high. Such a *Laya*-consciousness gives a balancing tone to the whole piece and creates a very lively atmosphere. To repeat, *Tala*, not only regulates but invigorates the musical performance.

The slow and fast *Laya* helps to produce diverse effects in music. For creating amorous, playful, wrathful and heroic moods, fast *Laya* is useful ; while slow *Laya* helps to produce feelings of tranquillity, devotion, seriousness and sadness. The medium *Laya* stands on the border line and may help to create either mixed feelings or the modulations of both the above groups of feelings.

In the type of music which utilizes the first group of *Talas*, the *Tala*-accompaniment gets predominance. The *Laya* being fast and the span of the *Tala* being short, it is easier for the artist to have ' cross-rhythm ' or ' to play with the *Laya* '. The *tabla*-player, in such a case, gets enough scope to exhibit his skill profusely — nearly on an equal basis with the main artist. The same is the case with instrumental music where the *Laya* is comparatively faster than in singing. On the contrary, in all types of serious music, which utilize the second group of *Talas*, the *Swara* gets the upper hand and the *Tala* recedes into the background unless, at times, the artist chooses to have ' cross-rhythm ' or ' to play with the *Laya* ' or in other words, the artist indulges in what is technically known as *Layakari*. In general, I may conclude that as music proceeds from classical to light varieties, the *Swara* gets less and less importance and the *Tala* gets more and more prominence. In the reverse course, the *Tala* goes into the background and the *Swara* comes to the forefront — about which we shall have to consider more in detail in the next chapter.[4]

---

[4] As *Tala* is one of the difficult aspects of Indian music, the teacher should, with the help of a *Tabla*-player, profusely illustrate the various technical terms, the difference between the idea of *Laya* and *Tala*, the different *Talas*, the three varieties of *Laya*, the importance of the non-musical sounds of the *Bayan* and so forth. I have coined some peculiar phrases like to ' catch the *Sama* ', ' get to a *Sama* ' ' playing with the *Laya* ', and others, the import of which should be clearly explained and illustrated. The reason why the *Talas* of the first group are easily understood and why difficulty is felt in the case of the other, should be thoroughly explained.

4. CLASSIFICATION AND VALUES

In popular parlance, Indian music is broadly divided into two main categories, Scientific and Light. Some use the term " Classical " instead of " Scientific ". But I do not think that the words " Classical " and " Scientific " are synonymous. Nor do I think the term " Classical " totally excludes light varieties. Of that, however, more later on.

These divisions being of comparatively modern times, we do not find any specific references, much less their definitions, in the old treatises. In modern times, many attempts to describe the import of these terms have been made. Scientific music, it is said, is one which strictly adheres to the rules of the *Raga*; while light music is that which does not so conform. But this description is faulty. There is many a *Raga Sangeet* (say, in *Patadeep, Tilang, Bageshri* and the like) which, while being within the rules of the *Raga*, is so rendered as to be easily styled as a light variety. Besides it is not true to say that all light varieties do away with the *Raga* rules. Then, it is said, that scientific music has an intellectual appeal while light music has an emotional appeal. This description is also not correct. To deny any emotional appeal to scientific music is to deny the very existence of its mood or *Rasa*. Likewise, to deny intellectual appeal to light music is to deny much of its vigour or vitality.

The conception of light music according to the common man, who does not give any serious consideration to music, or for that matter, to any other aspect of life, is, however, different. What is glittering and attractive at "first sight ", what he can easily understand and also imitate without straining himself either emotionally or intellectually, is according to him light music. All the rest is scientific. About classical music he has perhaps no occasion to think at all.

It may very well be questioned whether such a type of music should be classed as light or even music at all. Admitting the force of this objection, I may say, that I cannot afford to ignore this type of music which is cherished by a very vast majority of people and the production of which knows no bounds. I should, however, class this music under a separate heading namely, Limited Music. The span, the development, the appeal, the staying quality — everything in or about it is limited. Of this, I shall have occasion to add something more while dealing with different values and forms of music.

Reverting to the main classification of music, I must confess that to define what is scientific and what is light is not an easy job. The difficulty arises because the divisions are not watertight; nor are the connotations of the terms mutually exclusive. Barring border-line fusion, the distinction between the two classes is broad enough to be easily recognized. Scientific music, as the word itself suggests, is really one which remains strictly within the bounds of the rules of *Raga* : while the light varieties are often ' licentious '. It is equally true that the former appeals more to the intellect; while the latter to the emotion. Seriousness is the mainstay of the former; while the latter is predominantly light in character, as the word itself indicates. But it should never be misunderstood that what is unscientific is light and what is not light is scientific.

What makes the distinction between the two more marked is that the two classes materially differ in their aims and appeal and therefore in their approach too. The objective before the former is to rouse feelings of heroism, virility, awe and thrill and through this to attain tranquillity and sublimity. The other tries to rouse the feelings of mirth, affection, amorousness and yearning and through this to attain pathos and peace. If in the one, there is a more massive build, a larger sweep, a show of power, and a certain grandeur, in short, qualities which appeal first to the intellect, then in the other, there is a softness of lilt, delicacy and gentleness of appeal, an engaging tenderness and pursuasiveness — in short, qualities which have an easy and direct appeal first to the heart. These two types can, metaphorically speaking, be classed as the ' male ' and ' female ' varieties in music. Though diverse in character, both have strength, appeal and attraction in their own way. And here too, as is our experience, the instances of free ingress in each other's spheres, are not at all few.

Popularity of Light Music

Without pursuing the simile or the distinctive features of the two varieties further, one fact must be admitted, namely, that, of the two groups, light music is the more popular. This is evidently so

M 3

because light music kindles popular feelings and it has an ' attractive-first ' approach. Being largely free from the rigidity of rules and scientific forms, it has a lesser strain on your intellect. The use of a short span, popular themes and fast rhythm add to its attraction and intelligibility. It is thus a type of music which one can more easily understand and assimilate too. No wonder, therefore, that it should become more popular than the serious or scientific type.

Scientific music, on the other hand, has a serious job to perform. There is no smooth sailing. The path is difficult, weary and long. Like a human child, it takes a pretty long time to ' attain majority,' i.e., to assume any serviceable shape or form. On the contrary, the light variety, like the young ones of animals or birds, is quite attractive and serviceable even in its primary and early stages. Being so easy, short, and practical a pursuit, many an artist takes to light music — a factor which adds to its popularity.

Classical Music

So far, I have purposely avoided using the term ' classical ' instead of ' scientific '. My reasons are twofold. I think it would be doing injustice to the very high concept of the word classical, if all that passes under the name of scientific music is to be ranked as classical music. With due apologies to the champions of scientific music, I have to say that much of it is *merely* scientific, but not artistic. Music is primarily an art. The science of music, as that of any other art, cannot be an aim and end in itself; but must be only a means to achieve the artistic goal. Very unfortunately, emphasis is being given to the *means* to the detriment of the *end*, with the result that the scientific music, many a time, severs itself from the high classical standard. Another reason is that the partisans of scientific music, who place their music on a par with classical music, are not prepared to concede that status to light music. Here also, I have, humbly, to differ from them. Light music, if properly developed, does attain the height of classical music. If it were not so, the various forms of light music, like *Thumri, Tappa, Gazal* would not have formed part and parcel of our musical art; and the master artist would not have indulged in them at all.

But what is this classical music? It must be at once said that the concept of this highest goal of music is too complex to be explained, and too difficult to be understood. Like the highest conception of any other art, it is only to be realized or experienced.

The word classical has a slightly different meaning when used in a different context, such as literature, painting, etc. In music, too, the term as used with reference to Western music is not identical in its import when used with reference to ours. Our original word for it is *Abhijat* (of a noble class or of noble descent). Without going into these subtle differences, it would suffice that the average listener understands the word as meaning the highest or the best.

So far, I have discussed the chief values and elements in music. For example, a melodious cultured voice, proficiency in rendering *Alankaras, Tanas* and *Alaps*, etc. a thorough mastery over *Raga* and *Tala* systems and skilful presentation of all these, do constitute the chief values and· elements in music. But these alone, though they may serve as a very favourable background or preparation, would not suffice to produce real classical music. Classical music is not merely a bundle or admixture of all good elements in music. To attain classical excellence, what is most essential is the *Rasa,* the real musical content, or the emotional appeal.

The phrase 'emotional' appeal with reference to classical music, has to be understood, however, in a restricted but deeper sense. In its ordinary sense, emotional appeal is an appeal to the primary human feelings of joy, sorrow, amorousness and the like. To make an appeal to such feelings, is no doubt, the chief function of musical art. That is why I have referred to such feelings while describing the primary aims and appeal of scientific and light music. There, too, I have purposely used the word 'primary'; for the ultimate aim and appeal of both the types of music is the same namely, the, *Rasa-Siddhi* (establishing the *Rasa*). The meaning of this emotional appeal with reference to classical music — wherein there is fusion of scientific and light music — has a deeper import. The emotion here is pure and abstract, i.e., quite distinct or free from the actual feelings of joy, sorrow and the like. It would, no doubt, give you aesthetic joy or pleasure that is not tainted with materialism or utility. It would reveal to you a vision of beauty with which no material object can bear comparison. It would transport you to an elevated experience which is transcendental and in a sense supernatural. So the chief point of importance in classical music is this *Rasa-Siddhi*. If that is achieved, well, all that could be achieved in music has been achieved. Then, it does not matter whether the artist has all or some of the necessary qualities in music. It does not matter to what class (light or scientific) his music belongs, what form he resorts to, what *Raga* he chooses or what the poetical theme of the song is.

But, I am afraid, the lay listener would not get any appreciable idea of what is classical music by the above discussion. As said before, aesthetical concepts are to be understood by experience or realization alone. But when listening to a master artist the listener thinks himself to be elevated to a high plane, his sense of time is lost, the working of his analytical faculty is suspended and he enjoys a state of mental ecstasy, it may, then *fairly* be said that he is listening to classical music. I said ' fairly ' because such an experience must be that of a *Rasika* (a connoisseur), but must not be merely the infatuation of an impulsive person.[1]

The classification in music hitherto discussed can be conveniently stated by means of the following table :

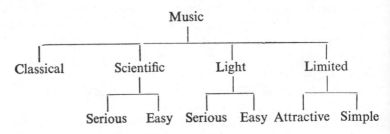

It should be noted, that ' classical ' is not a different class altogether. It is but the highest form of ' scientific ' and ' light '. The classification ' scientific — easy ' is popularly termed as ' light classical ' or ' *Sugama Ragdari* '. The classification ' Light — serious ' is sometimes called ' classical light '. Just as ' scientific ' and ' light ', the ' light ' and ' limited ' classes mentioned above are not absolutely watertight nor are they absolutely exclusive of each other.

---

[1] I am not, as is usual with me, giving any hints to the teacher as far as exhibition of classical music is concerned. An ordinary teacher is not expected to give such demonstrations. He should draw the attention of the listener to the master artists and their performance where, of course, they have attained such heights.

Values in Music

While dealing with voice-culture, *Alankaras*, *Raga* and *Tala*, we had to consider the essential values in music. Now let us inquire into some more.

Absence of a Drone Instrument

Music is generally rendered with the help of some instrument supplying the drone — the basis or fundamental note, say, a *tambura*, a harmonium, or even a simple *ekatari* (a single-wire device). In instrumental music the drone is supplied generally by the instrument itself. A common question is asked as to why such an assistance is necessary at all.

First of all, the importance of the idea of a drone should be clearly understood. The idea of a note itself *presupposes* some relation of it to the basic note. The tonic thus determines all other notes. The importance of the instrument which constantly supplies this note would be, therefore, very evident. It is this basic note on which you have to build your musical structure. It is this basic note which enables you to fix all the intervals of the other notes by means of comparison and contrast. If, therefore, one sings without such help of a drone, there is no fixity in his tonic. Necessarily there is no fixity for the other intervals; with the result that the whole tonal background and harmony of the music suffer. That is why some drone instrument is essential: and it need hardly be said that the better the instrument, the better it supplies the tonal background.

Short-span Music

An octave consists of seven main notes or, with variations, of twelve notes in all. Now the span of the full-fledged *Khayal* (the highest form in scientific music) extends not only to the full middle octave but to a few more notes both in the upper and the lower octave too, i.e., nearly two complete octaves. But there are thousands of *Geetas* (songs) which do not utilize the full octave even. For example the span of folk-music and of film-music does not extend beyond one tetrachord or so. Many a song of the light type, like *Gazal*, *Dadra*, *Bhava Geet*, etc. does not use also the full octave.

At any rate their range is smaller than that of a full-fledged *Khayal*. So, conveniently, for songs of this type, the tonic is raised to *Madhyama* by tuning the first wire of the *tambura* to *Madhyama* and treating the first wire as the basic note.

The advantages of the ' short-span ' music are twofold. It is easier to render and easier to follow and imitate on account of its short range and fewer complications. Its second advantage is that on account of the raised pitch of the tonic it becomes immediately impressive. Its main drawback is obvious from its short range itself. It does not admit of full development or full scope as a full-fledged type of music does. Therefore, much of the short-span music will have to be included in the ' limited ' class.

Improvisation and Improvisability

Every song is composed in some tunes and the singing of the song, at least, means singing of the whole text of the song with no variations or with very few variations. The composition of the bulk of folk-music, for example, is such that it does not admit, or does not expect, any improvisation thereof. Film-music is another variety of music which is completely pre-composed and which does not admit of any other improvisation than what little it has already. It is so composed and tuned that there is no scope for extempore development. So, if one wants to sing it, one has merely to reproduce it exactly in the way in which it is composed and end it where it ends. If one is enamoured by its tunes and wants something more of it, then one has only to sing it over again and stop where the composer stops.

It is quite obvious that this runs counter to the central idea of our musical development. Our music worth the name, must admit of improvisation, i.e., extempore development by way of tonal extensions, *Alaps*, *Bol-making*, *Tanas*, etc. How much one has to indulge in it is, of course, a matter which may vary according to circumstances. But extempore development is expected in all good music; and, therefore, the composition of a good *Geeta* must have the quality of ' improvisability '.

The Freedom of the Artist

That good music expects an extempore development of a song at once takes us to a very important feature of Indian music, namely that it gives a wide freedom to the artist. In the case of the pre-composed music of the Western type or of the Film, the artist — technically called the executant — who delivers the goods is a mere mouth-piece who reproduces someone else's music. This means that there is no freedom left to the executant. Needless to say that Indian music does not approve of this dissociation of the ' brain ' from the ' hands.' Here the ' creator ' is himself the ' executor '.

It is true, however, that many of our famous songs and *Cheezas* are pre-composed also and as far as possible the tunes of the old composition are maintained. But as our music does not end with mere reproduction of the *Cheeza* but really *starts* after its repro-duction, the artist has, further, full scope to show his ability and skill. Similarly that the artist has to sing a song in a particular melody or a *Tala*, is also no real restriction. *Raga* is just like a subject-matter or a theme for an essay which the writer is free to develop in his own fashion. *Tala* is a time-measure, no doubt, but it is not a time-limit. The artist can develop a piece for any length of time *provided* that he has something new to add and he keeps up the interest of the listener.

The most important effect of the freedom which an artist enjoys is the individual interpretation which we have through each per-formance. It is on account of this individual interpretation that we like to hear the same *Raga*, the same *Cheeza* over and over again. For, from each artist we get a different angle of the same picture. For, each time by his imagination and inspiration the artist gives the *Raga* a different colour. The freedom which the Indian system of music allows to an artist must be regarded as one of its most important values.

Emphasis on Bol or Swara?

We have seen that our music proper never ends with the singing of the mere words of the song; but some improvisation is also expected. This improvisation mainly consists of the *Alap* and the *Tanas*. *Alap* may be *Bol-Alap*, i.e., with the words of the song; or may be without it, i.e., with *Swaras* only. Similarly *Tanas* may be of two kinds : with the words, i.e., *Bol-Tanas* or with the *Swaras* alone. A question arises whether the *Gayaki* should be

Swar-Pradhan (*Swar*-dominating) or *Shabda-Pradhan* (word-dominating). To put it differently, whether, in developing a song, emphasis should be placed on the *Swara* element or on the *Bol* (word) element.

From this point, the *Gayaki* can be of four kinds : (1) completely of words, (2) predominantly of words, (3) predominantly of *Swaras*, and (4) without any words at all. Roughly speaking folk-music and film-music would form the first category; light music varieties like *Gazal, Dadra, Bhav-Geet*, etc. would form the second category; scientific music the third and instrumental music the last. On account of this difference, that is, the predominance of words or otherwise, the musical values of each category also differ. Hence the importance of the question.

In the music of the first two categories where words predominate, the meaning of the words, the poetical content, and the emotional appeal contained therein naturally come into prominence. The medium of making an emotional appeal of the song is, also, the words themselves of the song. Some are tempted to deduce from this that it is the words or the poetical content which is generally responsible for the aesthetic appeal in music. They further assert that scientific music where words do not play an important part, is not, therefore, favourable for attaining the artistic goal whereas light music does oftener attain that artistic goal.

There is another side to the problem. In the music of the third category where *Swara* element predominates and words are negligible, the emotional appeal is achieved mostly by means of *Swara*. Therefore, some others say, that it is the *Swara* element in music which is really responsible for attaining that goal. They further argue, that the essential elements of music are only two, *Swara* and *Laya*. It is, therefore, appropriate, that the emotional appeal in music should be dependent only on those essential elements and not on any other extraneous unessential element like the word. They go to the length of saying that light music where *Swara* does not play a predominant role, is not capable of emotional appeal as scientific music is. In short, this appears to be a controversy between the aesthetes who look upon music from the point of view of its pure musical value and *litteratuers* who do so from the point of view of its literary value.

Taking an impartial and unbiased view, certain positions will have to be accepted. First of all, to say that emotional appeal is not possible without the help of words, is an extreme proposition. If that were so, instrumental music, which is absolutely without any words, shall have totally to be denied any emotional appeal. To say, on the contrary, that words are not at all necessary for making an emotional appeal is equally an extreme statement. Singing without any words is well nigh an impossibility and certainly it would be dry and weary. That is why *Alaps* and *Tanas* are rendered with *Bols*. It is on account of the absence of words, that instrumental music also fails to sustain as much interest as vocal music does. The true position, appears to be that words are not *essential* but certainly *helpful* to make the emotional appeal. Therefore, songs which have a good musical and lyrical value are more conducive to attainment of the desired *Rasa*. But the other opinion, viz., that emotional appeal depends on words or lyrical content cannot be accepted. For an illustration, take the famous *Thumri* ' Piya Bin Nahi Awat Chein ', and instead of singing it in its usual *Khamaaj* tunes, attempt to sing it on the lines of ' Itane Joban ' or ' Gayiye Ganapati ' (both *Cheezas* in *Bhoop*) or on the lines of an oft-sung *Cheeza* in *Hamir* — and see the miserable effect. The listener would at once realize that the lyrical content and the peculiar emotional appeal, for which the said *Thumri* is known for several years past, would not save it from falling flat when sung in the new tunes suggested. We cherish that *Thumri* for the peculiar *Swara-Mela* (combination of notes) to which it is tuned and the way in which it is developed. Similarly hundreds of *Cheezas* are sung traditionally from generation to generation for hundreds of years, not on account of their poetical content or poetic appeal, but on account of their musical content and musical appeal. So, of the two elements, the *Swara* and the *Bol*, the former must be regarded as more responsible for creating the aesthetic appeal. Words are and must be there. But they are more or less like the vehicle for or conductor of the musical sounds. That is why, it is said that the glory of classical music does not depend on the words, the poetic theme or the *Bol*-making as it does on the *Swara-Vilas* or *Swara-Vistara* (improvisation or elaboration of notes).

From the point of view of musical values, it can safely be said, that as the *Bol* element in any musical piece goes on increasing or dominating, the intrinsic musical values of the piece go on decreasing. As a result, absolutely word-dominating *Gayaki* stands at a low level. On the contrary, the more a musical piece is freed from the ' word ' element and the more emphasis is given on ' *Swara* ' element, higher and higher becomes the level of that piece. But it should never be supposed from this that the best music should be devoid of any words or there should be any neglect of words. On the contrary, I would say that music must have words — words which are musically suitable and have an emotive value too. The artist should have a clear diction; he should never disregard the meaning of the words and should always endeavour to make use of the emotional content of the song to establish the *Rasa-Siddhi*.

The ' Law-abiding ' vs. the ' Licentious '

We have seen that certain *Ragas* do not maintain their prescribed melodic order throughout. I have classed such *Ragas* under the head ' Licentious ' (*Vide* chapter on *Raga* and *Tala*). These *Ragas* are few in number and they are only utilized in the forms of light music like, *Thumri*, *Dadra* and others.

The main advantages of using such *Ragas* is that by engrafting the melodies of other *Ragas*, an immediate ' change of moods '[2] is brought about. Necessarily such a change gives rise to a number of varieties and novelties and attraction for them is far easier and greater.

The artist who has to utilize the law-abiding groups of *Ragas* (i.e., where strict adherence to prescribed rules is necessary) has no such easy advantage. He has only one ' mood ' to explore; or has one ' colour ' at his disposal. His task in depicting various phases of one mood is, therefore, necessarily difficult like illustrating various shades and depths by means of only one colour. It requires creative imagination besides great ability and skill.

The *Ragas* of the above two types also have a different sort of appeal. Due to the ' licences ' one group takes, the appeal created by that group is bound to be superficially playful and flippant or at any rate lighter in character. The other group does not indulge in such licences; and hence its appeal is serious in character.

Considered from the point of musical values, it can be said that

[2] The ' change of moods ' referred to here is not the same as is understood by that phrase in Western music. By this change-over, one *Raga*-mood is substituted by another *Raga*-mood. The general melodic order is not at all changed.

strict *Ragadari Gayaki* stands on a higher level than one which uses ' licentious ' *Ragas.*

From what has been discussed above, it can be generally concluded that the simpler the song, the lesser is its musical value, so that at its lowest ebb (folk-music of the simplest type), the songs have practically no musical value at all. On the contrary, the more the musical values a song contains, the more difficult it becomes to render and to follow too.

Summary

For convenience, let me put, in a nutshell, my conclusions as regards the essential elements and values in music discussed so far :

(1) *Swara* and *Laya* are the two essential constituents of music. Indian music has also a third constituent, viz., the *Raga.*

(2) The musical scale is not an arbitrarily chosen scale. The importance of a drone and the importance of the *Shadja-Panchama* or *Shadja-Madhyama* relations should be clearly understood.

(3) The qualities of music vary with the qualities of the voice. So it is necessary to train the voice or to have ' voice-culture.'

(4) A note should not only be sweet but it ought to be musically fit. For musical fitness, mere natural qualities of voice do not suffice. The voice has, further, to be trained or cultivated.

(5) Steadiness, continuity, resilience and volume are a few other necessary qualities of a note. Above all, a note must be pleasing. In other words, *Aas, Kas* and *Rasa* are the essential qualities of a note.

(6) In embellishments, some are essential and some are merely ornamental. Similarly some are cheap and some are of high quality. Very judicious use of *Alankaras*, especially those which are merely ornamental and of cheap quality, must be made.

(7) *Gayaki* in which *Alapi* predominates is higher than one wherein *Tanabazi* predominates.

(8) Fast rhythm is not so much favourable for improvisation or elaboration or for generating the *Rasa* as the slow rhythm is. Musical heights are, therefore, generally attained in slow rhythm *Gayaki.*

(9) In music ' catching of the *Sama* ' is undoubtedly essential;

but the proficiency does not end with it. The *Gayaki* must exhibit a *Laya*-consciousness and *Layakari* too.

(10) Songs which utilize a full-fledged scale are of a higher order than those which utilize a part of the scale only.

(11) Songs, the tunes of which do not admit of improvisation or songs which are not improvised are limited in their character.

(12) The simpler the song, the lesser is its musical value. The more the musical values in a song, the more difficult it becomes to render and to follow too.

(13) *Swara*-dominating *Gayaki* stands on a higher level than the word-dominating one.

(14) The importance of the *Gayaki* of the ' law-abiding ' *Ragas* is more than the ' licentious ' ones.

These are, however, very general conclusions and I do not want to suggest that there are no exceptions to it. For the lay listener these conclusions would serve as broad tests to examine what are high and low orders in music.

5. MUSICAL FORMS[1] AND INSTRUMENTS

Folk-songs

OF ALL songs, folk-songs form the largest number. As the term *Loka-Geeta* suggests, it is the music of the masses and as such that music is widely spread among all the strata of society. Even the hill and forest tribes and the most backward communities have a rich heritage of such music.

Folk-songs can be divided into two groups. The first group consists of songs of the simplest type conceivable or of mere utterances with a crude cadence. These songs have various regional names which differ with each region. But though the names may differ and tunes may also slightly differ, the general level of that music is nearly the same everywhere. The recitation of hymns and prayers, poems set to metrical forms, domestic melodies, harvester's and reaper's songs, songs which relieve the tedium of labour, cradle songs, nursery rhymes, festival songs, play songs and several such ditties and croonings can be included in the first group. The bulk of it is the unwritten mass retained by memory and carried from mouth to mouth and from generation to generation. Nobody has purposely composed it or consciously tuned it. No voice-culture, no embellishments, no tonal extensions, even no rhythm and no skill whatsoever are required for its production. From the musical point of view, we need not consider this group at length.

In the second group of folk-songs devotional songs (light *Bhajans*) ballads, encomiast's compositions, occasional songs, erotic songs (like the *Lawani* of Maharashtra) and a host of other songs which are sung at some length, can be included. These songs do not generally employ the full scale of a *Raga*. But they employ melodies which can be traced to some *Raga* or the other. Their simplicity of musical composition and use of a few notes of an octave, make their rendering very easy. Rhythm is their mainstay — no matter by

[1]The word ' form ' is not used here in the sense of the various stages of any particular composition but as denoting the various types of music.

what instrument or by what simple means it is exhibited. These are songs where words, i.e., the poetical content predominates. As songs depicting lively, familiar and attractive subjects, the popularity of this group of folk-music is beyond question.

The *Lawani*, though a species of folk-music of Maharashtra deserves special mention. Its first attraction is the voluptuous and sexy themes it deals with. From the musical point of view, its design is more artistic, it is sung in a high pitch and is more capable of improvisation so that when master artists, perchance, handle it, the *Lawani* touches even the sphere of classical music. *Lawani* is, therefore, rightly styled as the Queen of Marathi *Loka-Geeta*.

The *Bhajans* and the *Quawalis* (which are, like *Bhajans*, the devotional songs of *Muslim* culture) are also types of folk-music, which admit of musical development at some length.

Leaving the above exceptional cases, when at times it is developed at length, folk-music in general is after all a ' limited ' type of music. That means its development, appeal and staying qualities, are all limited. Even so, the popularity of folk-music cannot be denied. It is really the music of the masses, is produced in the largest number and is practised by the greatest number of people. The simplicity of composition, easy imitability, themes of common experience and interest and the simple and fast tempo of the rhythm, account for its very wide popularity.

Film-music

I said that folk-music is the music of the masses and that it is the most popular; but I am afraid I shall have to amend my statement in view of film-music, the most captivating music for the young generation of today. At present, film-music has captured all the urban and semi-urban areas. But with the radio becoming popular in rural areas and with the prospect of the rural areas being supplied with electricity, the cult of film-music would not take long to capture the rural ears also.

Though I am classifying both folk-music and film-music under the same head, viz., ' limited ' (*vide* my classification in the last chapter), and though both of them are very popular, they materially differ in character and merits. The creation of one is quite natural. We don't know who composed it nor who gave the tunes. In the other, the formation, the composition and the music-direction

— everything is known; nay, it is purposely made known. On the one side, there is no gift of voice, no aid of accompaniment or of any other kind; on the other, you have the ' best voice ', a full battalion of accompanying artists and above all the resourceful Music Director. And as regards the propaganda and the technique of achieving popularity, you can't compare one with the other. It is not surprising, therefore, that the effect of the one should be quite unassuming and mild; and that of the other, very spectacular and ravishing !

A LIMITED MUSIC

From the point of view of musical art, film-music is a ' limited music' in every sense of the term, though certainly more attractive than its sister variety, folk-music. To begin with, the music lasts only for a few minutes. Deducting the time usurped by the ' introductory ' and ' side ' music, the main artiste hardly gets a couple of minutes. The main drawback, however, is that the artiste does not at all sing on his own, but merely reproduces the ' pre-composed ' or ' set-music ' of another. The inspiration, imagination and individuality for which we look in music, is conspicuously absent here.   And above all the absence of the human element.

Considering the ' pre-composed ' music on its merits, we see that it is music where no improvisations worth the name are attempted. It is music the end and aim of which is either to provide some merriment or to heighten the effect of a particular situation — that is quite a different aim from the attainment of emotional height or aesthetic pleasure for which all good music strives. With these deficiencies, film-music cannot be classed along with the scientific or light varieties proper. Besides, the growing tendency evidenced in the systematic disregard of the melodic rules of the *Raga*, and attempts to ' harmonize ' music on the lines of Western music, make it practically impossible to judge it by the standards of Indian music.[2]

However, serious thought has to be given to this music, as its

---

[2] I am aware that my remark may not hold good as regards many pictures in regional languages such as Marathi, Tamil, Bengali and Telugu wherein efforts to adjust music with *Raga* discipline are made. Similarly films like ' Tansen ', ' Baiju Bawara ', ' Jhanak Jhanak Payal Baje ', though in Hindi, serve as exceptions on account of the peculiar musical themes.

ever-growing popularity, especially with the younger generation cannot be ignored. Yes! ' evergrowing ' in spite of the adverse comments of the elder generation and the lovers of the classical music, and in spite of the official attempts of the All India Radio, to discountenance it. Yet, the onslaught of the flood of this music does not stop. On the contrary, Radio Ceylon, Radio Goa and the *Binaca Geet Mala* flourish vigorously on the enthusiasm of devoted listeners. Ultimately, it has captured homes, tea-shops, the streets, schools and colleges. Experience of annual socials of educational institutions will uniformly show how much juvenile artists of the educational world sing cine-songs; for, that is the only music appreciated by their audience. The All India Radio also had to yield and reintroduce film-music, of course, with a certain moderation and a change of name. The music which thus has come to stay and which has captured the public ear cannot be totally ignored and brushed aside as devoid of merits. Let us, therefore, examine its merits.

The songs of film-music can be grouped under three categories :

(1) Songs that conform at least to the melodic principles of the *Raga* system.

(2) Songs on which harmonization of Western music is grafted.

(3) Songs which follow no order or system and achieve nothing better than some awkward or hybrid effect.

About the innumerable songs of the third category, which die no sooner than they are born, I need not say anything. The question of popularity in their case does not arise; for, even the staunch cine-fans do not take any heed of them.

Some of the factors that go to give the songs of the first two groups a wide popularity are the following :

(1) Catchy tunes that immediately captivate the listeners ;

(2) Tunes that are readily understandable and easily imitable;

(3) The spectacular or novel background-music provided with the aid of various kinds of instruments;

(4) The selection of a play-back artiste gifted with a melodious, pointed and ' mike-suitable ' voice;

(5) Situation and the ' star ' connected with the song;

(6) Incessant attempts to find something new and novel;

(7) Special propaganda and spreading technique which ensures that the music always bangs on your ears in spite of yourselves; and

(8) Music for which you have to pay very little or nothing for that matter.

The very description of the merits of the film-music would disclose the deficiencies therein, to many of which I have already referred above. The foremost of them is the transient effect of the music. The effect of the new song is like the new incoming fashions in the market which throw the existing ones out of date ; or like the burning and hot news of the hour which becomes stale immediately the fresh news arrives. That is why ' *Apki Farmaish* ', '*Apki Pasand*' and ' *Chotika Geet* ' (all nearly meaning ' your choice ') is an ever-changing affair. Cine-goers always crave for something new and novel since what they already had, had exhausted its charm. For a moment, compare this state of affairs with the other classes of music. We have been listening to the same songs and their same melodies from generation to generation. Yet the songs and their music have not become stale; nor have our interest and attraction for them in any way diminished. The real work of art never becomes out of date. It always remains fresh. Its joy, therefore, as that of ' a thing of beauty, is a joy for ever '.

It is necessary to say a few words about the methodical attempts that are being made at grafting the principles of harmony of Western music on our music. The ' change of moods ' and the cumulative, powerful and variegated effect of the several instruments are the important features of ' harmony '. Attracted by these and having tremendous resources at their command, that the film-music directors should be tempted to make experiments in ' harmony ' with our music, is quite understandable. Cross-breed experiments are always so tempting. And taking into consideration some of their successful experiments, it must be said to their credit, that they have really shown ' what they can do ' even with such a foreign and incompatible element. But from the ever-growing tendency to make such attempts it is feared that what was started as an experiment in novelty only is being continued as a normal pursuit. What is more objectionable is that attempts to introduce very cheap and low varieties like ' rock'n roll ', ' yodelling ', which the lovers of Western music also despise should be made.

M 4

That the talented artists with tremendous resources and means and with the best ' voice ' at their command should produce such trash is really pitiable. And when one sees the devastating effects which such music creates on tender and impressionable minds; and when one sees that these youngsters sing, day in and day out, the tingling hits like ' Lal Lal Gal ', ' Ina Mina Dika ', ' C-A-T, Cat, Cat, Yane Billi ', ' Oh, Oh, Oh, Baby ', ' Mister John, Baba Khan ', ' Ye Dil Hai Mushkil ', ' Mai Rangila Pyar ', ' Ai Ai Ya Suku Suku ', ' Chahe Muje Koi Jangle Kahe ', ' Lal Lal Dekho ', — one feels very much depressed.

Fortunately, all film-music is not of the above type. Some of the songs of the first group which conform to certain accepted melodic principles, are really attractive.[3] Of course, these are very rare and they please because they come like oases. It is these songs which make me optimistic about the fact that film-music, if the ' persons concerned ' only will it, could be made to serve in its own way, the cause of real music. The discussions as to how this can be done could be deferred to the last chapter.

Thumri

Of all the types of light music *Thumri* must be regarded as the highest. This form embraces all the good qualities which light music stands for and in this sense *Thumri* can be said to be the parent or genus of all other forms of light music.

Thumri has first of all a lyrical value. The themes of lyric generally centre round *Shringar* (love) and its allied feelings of amorousness, affection, entreaty, yearning, pangs of separation, and the like. *Thumri* uses very few *Ragas* and that too of the ' licentious ' type like *Khamaj, Tilak-Kamod, Pilu, Kafi, Bhairavi, Jogi* and *Des,* in the development of which deviation from the strict rules of the main *Raga* and engrafting of suitable melodies from other *Ragas* are permissible. Great skill lies in this ' change-over ', so that the listener should derive the pleasure from the change of moods without any jolt whatsoever.

Another peculiarity of *Thumri* lies in the development of *Bols* (words) of the lyric. The lyrical content of the song is to be impressed on the listener. An artist cannot elaborate or elucidate his theme by means of words different from those of the song, as an orator

[3] Some instances are given in the last chapter.

would do, but has to do this by means of different notes. Thus by using different graces, ornaments and patterns of notes, he gives a sort of a different expression to the same words. This ' Bol-development ' which may also be described by phrases like ' ornamental Bol-filling ', or ' Bol-making ', is not only the important feature of Thumri singing but is the essence of all good types of light music for it is through this ' Bol-development ' that light music makes its emotional appeal. In other words, Bol-developing is to light music what Alapi is to the Khayal singing.

Unlike other types of light varieties, Thumri is sung in a comparatively slow tempo. The Talas used are usually Punjabi (used only for Thumri) and Deepchandi. Slow rhythm necessarily brings with it sustained and long-drawn notes giving a serious tone to the singing. This helps the Thumri to reach classical heights sooner than its sister varieties.

But it should not be supposed that the Thumri is all serious singing. The licence it takes with Ragas, the Bol-playing it indulges in, and, above all, the softness and tenderness which pervades all through its presentation, make the Thumri essentially a light variety. Added to this is the ' change of rhythm ' which Thumri singing has at the end of Antra (the latter part of the Cheeza) i.e. when the rhythm is doubled and the words of the ' burden of the song ' are woven into it with a variety of patterns. This change of rhythm serves as a relief to the otherwise slow tempo of the Thumri and immediately creates a lively and jubilant atmosphere.

Three different styles of Thumri-singing are in vogue. The Banarasi or the Poorab, the Lucknavi (of Lucknow) and the Punjabi. The Banarasi style is a bit serious and simpler in development than the Lucknavi. It indulges more in Bol-development and uses Meend and short Tanas. The Lucknavi style does not lay as much stress on Bol-development as the former and uses Khatka, Murki and short but cross Tanas.

The Punjabi Style

The Punjabi style of Thumri, however, is rather different in character as well as in form, from the first two styles. Unlike the two other styles, it does not much indulge in Bol-development, nor does it aim at seriousness. It uses Tanas peculiar to Tappa style of singing.

But the peculiarity of this style which influenced other forms of light music and to which the attention of the lovers of music was attracted, is still different. One of the rules of the *Raga* system is that the sharp and flat varieties of a note are not to be consecutively used. But the *Punjabi* style indulges in using such consecutive notes freely; so that almost twelve notes of the octave can be touched by this style. Another peculiarity of the *Punjabi* style is that there is an attempt to create an impression of changing the original tonic to another chosen note by a constant rest and emphasis on such other note. This unusual and novel method of singing, on account of its unexpected variations, engages the attention of the listener very quickly. It is pleasing too, if practised judiciously and for a while. But if one overdoes one's part, the music becomes flippant and makes the listener uneasy about it. On account of the attempt of changing over the tonic, the method becomes very slippery too; and there is no knowing when the artist may lose his control and be out of tune.

Thumri is the most difficult form in light music. Even amongst light-music singers, very few practise it and fewer still have a mastery over it. The average listener may not be very much familiar with *Thumri* songs.

Dadra and Gazal

As compared to *Thumri*, *Dadra* and *Gazal* are lighter varieties. The main difference between *Thumri* and these light varieties is that they are sung in fast tempo, i.e., in *Talas* like *Kerwa* and *Dadra* and they do not aim at seriousness as *Thumri*-singing does. Necessarily, embellishments of a lighter type are profusely used. *Punjabi* style of singing is often resorted to. Barring these differences, these varieties have nearly the same features which their mother *Thumri* has, such as *Bol*-development, taking liberties with *Raga*, having themes centring round love and allied feelings and making an emotional appeal to those feelings.

Gazal is necessarily a love-song in Urdu or Persian language. Its peculiarity is that after the burden of the song is over, the further stanzas of the lyric, which are termed as ' Shares ' are to be sung without the use of *Tala*. The idea underlying appears to be to draw the attention of the listeners more to the content of the lyric. *Dadra* varieties are so called because they are mostly sung in *Tala Dadra.*

Bhav-Geet

There are many other regional and seasonal varieties of light music which need not be mentioned except the *Bhav-Geet* of Maharashtra which has come into prominence in the last three decades or so. *Bhav-Geet* is a specially composed lyric, having an outstanding emotional and poetic appeal, which can be set to music. It is set to very attractive tunes and it is sung in *Talas* of fast tempo. Its *Gayaki* (singing) combines in it the trends of *Gazal*, *Dadra* and the popular light varieties established on the Marathi stage. Endowed with such a heritage, *Bhav-Geet* can be given a status next to *Thumri* in Indian music.

Tappa

This is one of the light types of music which is fast disappearing from the musical field. Unlike *Thumri*, *Tappa* does not indulge in *Bol*-making and is sung in different *Ragas* of the simpler type. Its speciality is the shaking of notes, cross pattern of *Alaps* and short *Tanas*, commencing with jerks, strewn with *Khatkas* and descending with steps. Though the *Tappa* is not in vogue, the *Tappa* style of *Tanas* has been adopted in a few other types of light music.

In conclusion, I may say that all light forms of music are essentially of a ' word dominating ' type. The rhythm is generally fast. The span used is usually not of a full octave. The *Ragas* used are of the ' licentious ' character, and if otherwise, they are few in number and of simple ' *Sugam Ragadari* ' type. A very melodious, clear, pointed and elastic type of voice is required. That is why women who are naturally endowed with such a voice, do better in this branch, than men. Ornaments and *Tanas* of light character only are rendered. The themes of the songs centre round the amorous and the light aspects of life. The method of presentation is quite different from that used for serious forms and so is the appeal which it makes.

Stage-music

Before dealing with the scientific forms of music, I must say a few words about the Stage-music which stands midway between the light and the scientific types of music. There are several regional languages of India and each language has its own Stage and each Stage has its own music too. But what I write hereafter is particularly with reference to the music on the Marathi Stage only, which deserves special mention from the point of view of musical development.

The Golden Age (1880–1930) of the Marathi Stage has long gone by. But the music which so thrived has not completely disappeared from the present-day Marathi Stage. At any rate, the *Natya Sangeet* (Stage-music) which came to be established under the exigencies of Stage-presentation still survives by itself and through other forms of music.

The Marathi Stage exhibits both the scientific and light types of music. I think there is no form of music which has not been tried on the Stage. All forms from the simplest metrical rhymes of *Sanskrit* poetry right up to the classical heights, were tried on the Stage. But the peculiarity of the Stage-music was that none of these forms was rendered on the Stage in its original fashion. All music was ' tempered ' or adjusted to suit the needs of the Stage. Thus in the case of *Ragadari* music, *Ragas* of popular appeal were predominantly selected in view of the general standard of understanding of the audience. Besides, the method of presentation and development was neither too simple or elementary to lessen the interest of the average spectator, nor too intricate or obscure to be unintelligible to him.

In selecting light music, too, neither the highbrow *Thumri* nor the voluptuous *Lawani* type of singing was adopted. In short, the *Natya Sangeet* bridged the gulf between the rudimentary folksongs and the complicated perfection of *Ragadari* music ; and created a sort of middle-class in the world of music. In a sense, the present-day nomenclatures ' *Sugam Sangeet* ', ' classical light ' and ' *Bhav-Geet* ' are all varieties which owe their origin to *Natya Sangeet* itself ; and this is sufficient to give an idea of the Stage-music.

But what is more important from the view point of our inquiry is the consideration of the objectives which the persons responsible for the *Natya Sangeet* had and the effect it created on the public. To please the average theatre-goer was certainly the primary object. Not less important, was the object of creating amongst the general public a taste for good music. That is why the persons responsible for Stage-music never became mere tools in the hands of the public, by supplying what was demanded. On the contrary, they first decided what the public *should* have and then supplied it in a way which was both interesting and instructive. Through the Stage-music, the average spectator got himself acquainted with simple *Ragadari* music and various forms of light music. Thus the Stage not only gave a new direction to music but was also responsible for popularization of the musical art and for the outstanding growth of musical appreciation too.

If we pause here a little, and just consider what happened on the Screen, that powerful rival to the Stage, we are filled with pity when we discover that film-music did not give any substitute worth the name, but, on the contrary, adversely affected Stage-music. With the decline of the Stage, the progress of Stage-music was naturally arrested. What is worse is that the present-day Stage-music is also showing the tendency to follow in the footsteps of film-music. The music director is getting an upper hand on the Stage. The freedom hitherto enjoyed by the actor-singers is being checked considerably. The music given is of a light type. *Bhav-Geet* appears to be the highest target of music. The back-ground music, the side-music and the band or orchestra have made their way to the Stage — factors which further swamp the Stage-music. I have also witnessed some experiments in play-back-singing made on the Stage. I cannot imagine what more things the future has in store.

In spite of this, the Marathi Stage still retains its grip on the minds of the music-lovers. The taste which the people have thus acquired for genuine music, constantly takes them back to such old plays as ' Soubhadra ', ' Manapamana ', ' Swayamvara ', ' Ekach Pyala ' and others. They never seem to tire witnessing the same plays and listening to the same music over and over again. For the pleasure derived from pure and higher music is always an endless pleasure.

Dhrupada and Dhamar

With *Dhrupada* and *Dhamar* we enter the region of scientific music proper. Though *Dhrupada* form of music held the ground for over five centuries, it is fast disappearing since last forty years and is now almost extinct. Fixity, as the word *Dhruva Pada* itself suggests, is the guiding factor of *Dhrupada*. The notes, words, time-beats, everything is fixed. No embellishments, flourishes, *Tanas*, etc. are allowed. The real freedom appears to be in the cross-rhythmic movements of the words of the composition. The composition has four parts. They are so tuned that they give a complete picture of the *Raga*. The *Dhrupada* is necessarily sung in a slow tempo and uses only few *Talas*. Its importance lies in the fixity, purity and the long, sustained notes.

Dhamars are songs sung mostly during the *Holi* festival. It is called *Dhamar* for it is sung in *Dhamar Tala*. It uses a few more graces than the *Dhrupada* but in other respects it resembles *Dhrupada* and is almost out of vogue now.

Nom-thom

Though *Dhrupada* has gone out of the field, the peculiar *Alaps* — *Nom-thom* — which preceded and supplemented the *Dhrupada* still lingers a little. As *Dhrupada* admitted no scope for *Alaps* proper or other variations, it was thought necessary to supplement it with certain *Alaps*. As *Alapi* without any words would sound bald and lifeless, some words like *Nom-Thom*, *Whrom*, *Rheem* and others which have no meanings of their own, came to be used. In another sense, the *Nom-Thom* can be compared to the prelude-like *Alap*-making resorted to in some instrumental music like that of *sarod*, *sitar*, etc. Thus *Nom-Thom*, unlike *Alaps* in *Khayal*, is sung without any *Tala* accompaniment, though there is a sort of flow of *Laya* in it. Through *Nom-Thom*, the full structure of *Raga* can, no doubt be exhibited. But due to the meaningless and somewhat harsh words and due to the absence of *Tala* accompaniment, the *Nom-Thom* does not sustain interest. It is going out of fashion and very few artists make use of it now.

Khayal

Khayal is the highest type of scientific music of the present times and is the most dignified of all the forms of music. As it came as a reaction against the austere and rigid *Dhrupada*, its origin is comparatively of a later period, say, about three hundred years ago. *Khayal* means literally ' thinking ' or ' imagination.' And as a more thoughtful and imaginative form of music, it justifies its name.

Khayal is bound by the rigid rules of the *Raga* as the *Dhrupada*.

But in all other respects it differs, nay, improves on the *Dhrupada*. It makes free use of *Alaps*, *Bol*-developing, *Bol-Tanas*, *Tanas* and *Layakari* and in so doing utilizes appropriate *Alankaras* such as *Meend*, *Ghasit*, *Gamak*, grace-notes, etc. In short, the artist has absolute freedom of improvisation in this form.

Khayals are of two types : *Bada* (big) and *Chhota* (small) *Khayal*. *Bada Khayal* is necessarily sung in a slow tempo and in *Talas* suitable to it ; while the *Chhota Khayal* — also called as *Drut* — is sung in a fast tempo and in *Talas* suitable to it. The *Alankaras* used for the latter kinds of *Khayals* are of a lighter type. The method of presentation also differs a little with the two kinds. Necessarily, they vary in their appeal. The former creates seriousness and appeals to virility, wonder, sublimity and tranquillity. The latter, however, creates a rather lively atmosphere and appeals to playfulness, heroism, joy, anger and the like.

The *Cheeza* (song) has two parts.[4] The first part which is called *Asthai* includes the *Mukhada* (face), i.e. the burden of the song or the first line or the opening phrase of the lyric. The *Mukhada*, being the face, is the best part of the song. It has the choicest of tunes. It is indicative of the ' character ' of the *Raga* and the ' species ' of the form. It is this *Mukhada* which is to be repeated frequently as it contains the letter of stress (tuned generally to the dominant note) which has to coincide with the first beat of the *Tala*, i.e., the *Sama*. The importance of *Mukhada* is so much that to render it artistically and skilfully is tantamount to ' winning half the battle ' of the song.

The *Antara*, the latter part of the song, usually exhibits the notes of the particular *Raga* as contained in the second tetrachord. The ' letter of stress ' or the ' *Sama* point ' in the *Antara* is generally tuned to the upper tonic. That necessarily helps the artist to develop notes of the upper octave. The *Antara* is, therefore, resorted to after a sufficient ' warming up ' of the voice so as to sustain the high-pitched notes.

The process of development of a *Cheeza* is generally like this : (1) The recitation of the composed *Cheeza*, at least, its *Asthri* part. Some begin with *Nom-Thom* and then recite the *Cheeza*; (2) Slow-motion development of the *Asthai*, i.e., *Alapi*, both with the help of *Swara* and words ; (3) *Antara* and its development; (4) Then

---

[4] The songs of other forms also have similar parts. Therefore the discussion that follows would equally apply to other forms of music.

after increasing the tempo of the *Laya*, again *Alapi* and then *Bol*-making and *Bol-Tana*, and (5) last, the *Tanas*.

A glance at the summary of values in music given at the end of the last chapter will reveal that *Khayal Gayaki* comprises nearly all the values so enumerated. Thus, it observes the rules of the *Raga*, uses a full-fledged octave, is essentially a *Swara*-dominating and *Alap*-dominating *Gayaki* and is generally sung in slow motion, giving ample scope for all sorts of development. But amongst these, however, *Alapi* is the most important feature of *Khayal Gayaki*. I have already said that the function of *Alapi* is primarily to unfold the *Raga* scheme; and through it to attain the *Rasa-Siddhi* — the ultimate goal of music.

As in *Thumri*, there are various styles or schools of *Khayal Gayaki*. Such a school is known by the word *Gharana*. Of this, however, more in the next chapter.

A *Bada* (big) *Khayal* is usually followed by a *Chhota* (small) *Khayal* in the same *Raga*. This *Chhota Khayal* is necessarily sung in fast rhythm, which relieves the tension created by the serious mood of the *Bada Khayal*. Thus with profuse *Bol*-making, with the use of light *Alankaras*, and by cross-rhythm or ' playing with the rhythm,' it presents the lighter side of the same *Raga* picture.

Tarana consists of a set of peculiar words like *Dir, Tan, Tanana, Deem*, etc. which like *Nom-Thom*, have no meaning of their own. The peculiar succession of such words helps to make the diction clear.

Saragama is another variety of *Chhota Khayal* which uses the solfa passages or as the name suggests, the abbreviated names of the notes such as Sa, Ri, Ga, Ma, etc. Sometimes *Alapi* and *Tanas* are also rendered in *Saragama*. *Tarana* and *Saragama* owing to their meaningless words do not sustain interest for a long time, and are used very rarely.[5]

Not the Form but the Content......

But when all is said and done about various forms and their compara-

---

[5] The teacher should explain and illustrate all the varieties in scientific music. The difference between the method of presentation of a *Bada Khayal* and a *Chhota Khayal* should be clearly brought out. The various styles of *Alapi, Bol-Tana* should also be illustrated. The importance of *Mukhada* of a *Cheeza* should be properly exhibited.

tive excellence and values in music, I cannot but repeat that it is not the ' form ' but the ' content ' that matters most in musical art. Devoid of content, no form of whatever height or glory would save a musical piece from degenerating. Take, for example, the case of *Khayal Gayaki*. I have said that the *Khayal* is the highest and the most dignified form of music. But does the *Khayal Gayaki*, as commonly heard, bear testimony to it ? I am at great pains to say that much of it is meticulous observance of *Raga*-grammar, a mathematical display of *Tal*-beats and an exhibition of ' laboured skill ' or a show of dexterity. Science and acrobatics appear to be their motto. This is why I was not prepared to treat, as the readers must have observed in the last chapter, the scientific music on a par with classical music. The same is the case with light music. Unfortunately the word ' light ' has been so *lightly* taken by the persons concerned that anything — a tickling variety, a passing show — having some sensuous appeal passes for light music. Even in rendering *Thumri*, *Gazal* and *Bhav-Geet* — the higher forms of light music — we find that the artist's craze is for finding oblique patterns, dazzling novelties, flippant varie-ties, new tunes and new lyrics. In short, novelty appears to be their motto. We talk about the artist's imagination, intuition, inspiration and his emotional urge. But, I think, all these are conspicuous, more or less, by their absence only. Then, we hear about the ' aesthetic pleasure,' ' the vision of beauty,' the transcendental and mystic experience,' ' the self-oblivion ' and ' the self-elevation.' Do we experience anything of such sort ? What I want to stress is that music would not thrive as a musical art if it only cares for the form, the pattern, the dexterity, the novelty, the science and the like. Above all, it must aim at *Rasa-Siddhi*, the ultimate goal of music, more of which in the next chapter.

Instrumental Music

So far, I have said nothing in particular about instrumental music. Our instrumental music is also a very much developed music and is as old, perhaps, as vocal music itself. But it has always held vocal music as its ideal; and its general development and ideology does not materially differ from vocal music. To put it more emphati-cally, I may say that every instrumentalist is first a vocalist. When he plays, he really sings through his instrument. In this view, instrumental music can be rightly described as 'song without words'.

But even so, instrumental music differs from vocal music in point of details mainly on account of their various media of expression which are obviously different from the vocal chords. As each instrument differs in kind and construction, so the method of playing of each instrument also differs from the others. I do not, however, propose to enter into the details of their construction or of their method of playing but would make a few general remarks as regards their musical values and peculiarities.

In point of sound production, string instruments have certain advantages. We would see, when dealing with the *Tambura*, that a plucked wire simultaneously registers along with its main note its upper partials also. Resonance is also assured in these instruments by means of the hollowness of the gourd or the wooden frame and *jawari* mechanism. Besides, a number of ancillary wires suitably tuned are provided so that they help to create a harmonious background. But all the same it is a sound without 'life' and hence it cannot equal the human voice.

The instruments can be grouped into two groups: (1) string instruments and (2) wind instruments.

String instruments can be further divided into two classes : those played with stroke of fingers or plectra and, those played with the bow. *Veena* (which is also called *Been*), *rabab*, *sarod* and *sitar* belong to the former class ; while *sarangi, dilruba* and violin belong to the latter class. The former are used for solo-playing, while the latter are mainly used as accompaniment. *Veena, sitar* and *dilruba* have frets while others are without frets.

In case of instruments which are played with fingers or plectra such as *veena, sarod*, etc. no continuous sound is produced as is produced in bow-instruments but sounds are produced in jerks or strokes. These instruments are not, therefore, suitable for accompaniment. First of all *Alapi* on the lines of *Nom-Thom* is produced and then the instrument is played along with *Tala* accompaniment. *Khench, Ghasit, Meend* and grace-notes are the special features of all the string instruments.

The bow instruments (*sarangi, dilruba* and violin), on the contrary, give a continuous flow of sound and are, therefore, more suitable for accompaniment. *Sarangi* resembles the human voice (especially that of woman) and hence it is commonly made use of by songstresses.

Shehanai and *basari* (flute) are the two important wind instruments. But as they have no speciality in sound production as the string instruments have, they have not gained equal status with the latter class of instruments.

Tabla, its counterpart *dagga* or *bayan* and *mridang* are skin-percussion-instruments. Though they are, primarily, meant for *Tala* accompaniment, they are played also independently. As these instruments produce but one note, playing on them, unlike other musical instruments, cannot reproduce vocal music at all. They however, exhibit the art and science of *Tala* which has an independent existence in musical production.

6. MISCELLANY

EVERY art has its own problems. But as music is one of the most intimate expressions of human life, the problems of no other art are so widely discussed as those of music. The topics are, however, miscellaneous. Some have scientific interest; while others are of general interest only. A few relate to the actual performance; and a few others have become the subject of hot controversy also. In the succeeding pages, therefore, it is proposed to discuss some important topics about which an average reader should know something. Needless to say, in so doing, I shall not tax the readers with a purely scientific discussion.

The Time-table of Ragas

Any one who is somewhat familiar with Indian music, knows that there are certain restrictions as regards the singing or playing of particular *Ragas* at a particular time or hour of the day or night. To sing a morning melody at night or an evening melody at dawn is considered as *Nishiddha* (prohibited), as the singing of a prohibited note itself in a *Raga*. The question arises whether there is any basis, scientific or otherwise, for such an observance.

That such an observance has been in vogue for a very very long time cannot be disputed. Not only was a particular time or hour allotted to each *Raga*, but even certain *Ragas* were to be used only in certain seasons. But during the course of time, this seasonal restriction has not survived. As regards the time allotment also, many a change has taken place, that is, melodies which were formerly sung in the morning are now sung in the evening and *vice versa*. In spite of these changes, some definite time-table of *Ragas* is being observed and has persisted to this day. The question of its propriety and its basis has to be considered.

In current practice, there are various classifications of *Ragas* from the standpoint of particular divisions of time and attempts to deduce rules therefrom are made. Thus there are *Poorvang Ragas* and *Uttarang Ragas*. The *Poorvang Ragas* are sung from midday to midnight, while *Uttarang Ragas* are sung from midnight to midday. It is discovered that the *Vadi* (dominant) note in the former is in the first tetrachord. From this it is deduced that such a *Vadi* gives an ascending tendency to the *Raga* which is very suitable to the active part of the day when such melodies are expected to be sung. As regards the latter group of *Ragas*, whose *Vadi* is in the second tetrachord it is, likewise, said that the tendency of such *Raga* is descending which is suitable for the calm hours of night. There is also a group of *Sandhiprakasha Ragas*, i.e., *Ragas* to be sung at dawn and dusk which take Ri and Dha flats. The peculiarity of the evening twilight melodies is that they take F sharp, a note which is supposed to work as a change-over from day-time melodies to the night-time melodies. The broad characteristics of melodies of other hours also are found out and some justifications for them are also given.

But with due credit to the ingenuity of those who have been at pains to find out some significance in the existing time-table of *Ragas*, and while admitting that their conclusions may hold good for some *Ragas*, it must be said that there is no real and tested scientific basis for the whole system of existing *Ragas*. The *Ragas*, as said before have changed their hours. In the present-day order exceptions to the rules are innumerable. The same *Raga* (i.e., its equivalent) is sung at different times in the Northern and the Karnatak system. The *Shastrakaras* themselves allow the freedom to sing any melody at any time on the Stage or at the ' dictation of the King '. It is said that some melodies are to be sung at a particular time because the effect at that time is the greatest, in view of the mental attitude of the listener at that particular hour. Here, too, the matter appears to have had a subjective approach rather than an objective one. We have heard many a melody sung on the Stage irrespective of their conventional proper time. But it has never been our experience that on account of the wrong time the melody has not had the desired effect. This is why it is difficult to accept the old *Raga Samaya* (time) theory fully in the present state of affairs. Either the theory must be radically amended or the present-day time-table of *Ragas* must be completely overhauled.

But I do not subscribe to the view of the revolutionaries who are out to do away with all such restrictions. They say that if the system has no real scientific basis, why not break with it. I think that this is a wrong approach to the subject. He who wants to deviate from an established practice has to justify his action. After all, the system has been in vogue for a very very long time. It has, therefore, gained the sanction of an established *convention* at least. We have been accustomed to hear, for instance, the melody of *Bhairav* in the morning only and that of *Pooriya* in the evening. But if these melodies are sung at a wrong hour, then it does jar on our ears. Do we not observe so many conventions in our different walks of life? After all is said and done, conventions have a real significance in the decorum of life and in the art of living. A radical innovation and a whimsical departure are bound to invite a protest, not only from practitioners and connoisseurs of art but also from common listeners.

Harmony and Melody

The listener is already familiar with the terms Harmony and Melody, as they are used mainly to show the distinction between the Western music and our music. Since Indian film music began to make profuse experiments with harmonization, the words have not only come into prominence but have also become a matter of 'grave concern' to the lovers of Indian music. The listeners must know what all this is about.

The idea underlying Harmony, which is the mainstay of Western music, is to produce an effect by means of more than two notes rendered *simultaneously*. This is done by means of chords of three or more selected notes (say, CEG and GBDF), played on one or more instruments. The idea of Melody, on which Indian music mostly depends, is, however, to produce an effect by means of notes rendered *successively*. In other words, the emphasis, in one system, is on simultaneous combined effect of notes; while that in the other is on the succession of notes.

If we take into consideration this fundamental difference between the two ideologies, the reasons why Indian music did not or does not adopt Harmony as its basis will become evident. We have already seen, that in our system vocal music plays a dominant role. Instrumental music is merely a reproduction of it.[1] Now,

---

[1] Even when a singer is accompanied on a *sarangi* or a harmonium, the accompanying artist is supposed to give a 'follow-on' or a 'run-after-type' of accompaniment. Sometimes he may 'suggest' or 'prompt'; but all this is 'within the *Raga*'; and never by way of providing Harmony as technically understood.

it is quite evident that the human voice is able to produce only one note at a time. It is but natural that our music should develop on the principle of Melody and not on the principle of Harmony which necessarily requires more than one individual to produce different chords or notes simultaneously.

Another important consideration is that the *Raga* system, the unique and indispensable feature of our music, is but an order developed and evolved from the principle of Melody itself. In Harmony, prohibited notes are bound to be produced; which means an obvious violation of the rules of the *Raga*.

These two basically different conceptions of the two systems are responsible for many other points of difference between them, in form, development and effect. Let us take the instance of the values of the note. In Harmony, as more notes have to be produced simultaneously, the question of the true pitch of an individual note does not assume as much importance as it does in melodic order, which has to depend on the interval-effect of a note. That is why Western music remained satisfied with the ' tempered scale ' which our system did not tolerate. For the same reasons, Western music tolerates also the " bald " unadorned note. In our music notes are usually embellished by touches or graces of adjacent notes. So also is the case with other values of the note, the intricate *Shruti* scale and elaborate system of ornamentation. I may further say that no other system of music has paid such a minute attention as our system has to the nuances of the human voice, which when trained is richer than the tones even of string instruments. So our advance in *vocal* music at least has no parallel elsewhere.

Western music not only depends on the combined effect of notes but also on the combined efforts of different individuals, viz., the Composer, the Conductor and the Executant — in that order. In this hierarchy of artists, there is a sort of bifurcation of ' creation ' from ' execution ' or of the ' brain ' from the ' brawn '. The discipline is that each succeeding participant has to work under the strict directions of the preceding one with the result that the artist who actually produces the music, or delivers the goods, usually becomes no better than a skilled artisan. In our music, the ' performer ' is also the ' creator '. His only restrictions are those of the form and the scale which he has chosen to develop. Really speaking these cannot be called limitations at all. It is just like an author or an orator selecting a theme for his performance. Within those

M 5

bounds, however, our artist is absolutely free to develop his theme according to his ability and skill. As such he is not merely a mouth-piece which reproduces what is already ' pre-composed ' or merely an artisan who builds what is already ' prefabricated '.

Ever since experiments in Harmony came to be freely made in Indian film-music, these words which were hitherto used only for comparison, have assumed the controversial form of Harmony *versus* Melody. In spite of the apparent success it seems to achieve in that field, it must be said that Harmony has not gained an inch in Indian music proper. I doubt whether it will do so even in future. If our music is to be truly Indian, it must remain within its own bounds and must progress on lines suitable to it, but not on lines which would altogether change its character.

As I have no first-hand knowledge of the Western system of music I refrain from making any comparisons between the two and from suggesting that the one is either inferior or superior to the other. To do so would be outside the scope of this book also. My object in this discussion is only to emphasize that whatever may be the merits of Harmony *vis-a-vis* Western music, it is quite unsuited to Indian music as such.

Ban on Harmonium

It would be in the fitness of things if I take up the topic of har-monium after having dealt with Harmony. The former word is the derivative of the latter and harmonium is one of the instruments which is suitable for producing Harmony. But the reason why I am dealing with this topic is somewhat different. It is interesting to note that while attempts are being made from one end to intro-duce the foreign idea of harmony into our music, the instrument which has become part and parcel of our musical paraphernalia is being expelled from the other. The instrument has been in use in India for approximately less than a century. Though a few veteran artists avoided making use of it even for the purpose of accompani-ment, it must be admitted, that no other musical instrument is being used in this country on a wider scale than the harmonium. But the matter attracted public attention since All India Radio banned its use on its stations. The listeners must know, therefore, why on the one hand the instrument has attained such popularity and why it has invited official displeasure on the other.

The instrument is undoubtedly a foreign innovation. But its use is not banned only on that score. Other foreign instruments such as the violin and clarinet have made their way into our system without any protest. The objections against the use of the harmonium are chiefly two. First of all, the notes which the instrument produces are not properly pitched. We have seen that all notes bear a certain relation to the tonic. Now it is possible to tune the harmonium to a given tonic. If that is done, the harmonium cannot conveniently be used for any other note as tonic, for such a tuning would disturb the intervals of all other notes in relation to a different tonic. In order, therefore, that the instrument may be suitable for any note, the pitch of the majority of notes had to be ' compromised ' or ' tempered '. So with the exception of the Fifth note (or its complement the Fourth), which is nearer to the correct pitch, all other notes are defective.

Another defect in the instrument is that ornaments like *Meend, Ghasit, Gamak* and others which can be rendered easily by means of all stringed instruments, cannot be so rendered on the harmonium. The harmonium has only ' fixed ' notes. So there is no possibility of touching any *Shruti* in between. Thus harmonium-playing is striding from note to note instead of smooth gliding — a point very important for our musical art.

In spite of these inherent defects and in spite of the official ban the harmonium has captured the Stage, the School, the Home and the popular ear too. The majority of artists also accept it as an accompanying instrument. The reasons are not far to seek. The instrument has many ' saving qualities '. It does not require any tuning of wires, turning of pegs or changing of frets. It need not be changed with the individual. It suits any range of voice. It gives an ' ever-ready ' service. Press the key and it produces the sound. It is easier to play, most convenient to handle and suited to every pocket. From this practical point of view no other musical instrument can equal it. Leaving aside the case of a few artists who can afford to have the *sarangi* or violin as their accompaniment, all other artists have to depend on the harmonium, as there is no other suitable substitute for it. And what about those thousands of persons who are not able to produce notes even as nearer to the pitch of the tempered scale? If such persons follow the harmonium, a tempered scale at least is assured.

It should not be misunderstood, however, that I am advocating the cause of the harmonium. What I want to point out is that we cannot close our eyes to the relative merits of the instrument which has survived all odds. The proper remedy is not to ban it but to reform it. On this particular topic I would like to draw the attention of the persons interested to the fact that, in India, a harmonium which provides an additional variation for each note has been invented. (The author has himself seen the successful working of such a harmonium.) For this some extra buttons have been provided and the original arrangement of the Keyboard has not been disturbed. This makes it possible to have twenty-four notes (instead of twelve) in an octave so as to adjust the nearest correct note for any tonic and for any scale. The deficiency in the instrument arising on account of the ' tempered scale ' is thus removed to a great extent. If more research is made in this direction and proper aid is received, such a special harmonium can be manufactured and made commonly available.

I would never advise the students of music to learn music with the aid of the harmonium, for this would affect their sense of correct pitch. The artist should also avoid its use and prefer a string instrument for accompaniment. The harmonium is not a really suitable instrument for solo-playing. It should not, as far as possible, be used even to supply a drone. It can never be a substitute for the *tambura*, the real Indian drone.

Tambura

Tambura is a four-wired instrument with a big gourd at the bottom and a long hollow wooden neck above. The wires rest on two bridges, generally three feet apart, and they are adjusted by means of pegs at the top. The resonance of the sound, created by the hollowness of the gourd and the neck above, is enhanced by means of the shreds of wool or silk inserted between the wire and the lower bridge. The two middle wires are tuned in unison to any desired pitch, which serves as the basic note. The first wire is generally tuned to a lower fifth[2] and the last is tuned in unison with the fundamental note an octave lower.

[2] The first wire of *Tambura* is sometimes tuned to *Madhyama* when the artist wants to raise the tonic to suit musical pieces which do not utilize the full octave. When the first wire is tuned in this fashion, the middle two wires supply naturally the *Panchama* notes, in relation to the first note. In *Ragas*

On account of the huge size of the *tambura* and the delicacy of the fragile gourd, the instrument is very inconvenient to handle. It is also difficult to tune properly. But despite these handicaps, the instrument is being consistently used as a drone by our artists since the time of the known history of Indian music. It would therefore be worthwhile to see the reasons for this.

First of all, it is a string instrument. The science of acoustics has revealed that a stretched string when plucked not only produces the sound to which it is pitched, but produces simultaneously many more sounds which bear a fixed relation to its primary sound. It first vibrates in its entire length which produces its prime note. It also vibrates in two segments giving rise to a note twice as high as the prime; this again, in three segments producing a note three times higher; fourthly in four segments, giving a note four times higher and so forth. All of these motions are simultaneous. The first lowest note, i.e., the prime note, is the loudest and makes a first impression on the ear. The higher pitched notes, which are technically called as ‘ upper partials ’ or ‘ harmonics ’, are less and less audible. There, too, the upper partials which are but higher octaves of the prime (that is double, four times, eight times and so on) are not discernible on account of their complete unison; but other upper partials (such as three times, five times, etc.) are discernible to a trained ear. That is why when the first and fourth wires of the *tambura* are properly tuned we hear, though faintly, Ri and Ga notes respectively.[3]

The *tambura* not only supplies the prime notes and its Fifth but it supplies so many other notes of consonance through its upper partials — all of which provide a tonal background for the artist. With the aid of the prime notes, the artist is able to fix the true harmonic intervals of all other notes by means of comparison and contrast. On account of such peculiarities and unique features, the instrument has survived the test of time and can be considered to be the Emblem of Indian music.

where *Panchama* is prohibited and *Nishad* predominates, the first wire is tuned, by some artists only, to *Nishad* to heighten the effect of that note.

[3] The third upper partial of lower (G) $(180 \times 3 = 540)$ is double of D $(270 \times 2 = 540)$ and the fifth upper partial of lower octave $(120 \times 5 = 600)$ is double of E $(300 \times 2 = 600)$.

The Shrutis (Microtones)

So far we were considering the octave as consisting of twelve notes only. But our artists and scientists went further and made a very amazing discovery of no less than twenty-two notes in an octave. In an octave consisting of twelve notes, we have seen that each of the notes Ri, Ga, Ma, Dha and Ni have one variation each. According to the discovery of *Shrutis*, two more minute but audible musical notes such as *Ati Komal Gandhara*, i.e., note little lower in pitch than *Komala Gandhara* and *Tiwra Tara Gandhara*, i.e., note little higher in pitch than *Shuddha Gandhara* were discovered. So instead of two, the *Shruti* scale gives four varieties of *Gandhara*. Similar minute variations of other notes were discovered making thus a total of twenty-two notes in an octave.

It must be admitted, however, that the distinction between the *Shrutis* being very subtle and minute, an ordinary artist finds himself unable to produce these notes of minute variations. Even the master artist cannot exhibit all the different *Shrutis* successively. But it should not be supposed that the discovery has only an academic value. In actual practice, the master artists do produce such minute notes, whenever in any given *Raga* such differentiation becomes necessary. For example, the *Komal* Ga in *Kafi* and *Komal* Ga in *Todi* are not of the same pitch. The latter is softer and lower in pitch than the former. Similarly, the Dha of *Bhoop* is a little lower in pitch than the Dha of *Marwa*. The use of *Shrutis* is also made while rendering *Alankaras* like *Meend*, *Ghasit*, *Gamak*, etc. where the micronotes, in between the main notes, have necessarily to be touched.

I have already stated that it is difficult for the artists even to render a ' sharper ' or ' flatter ' variation of any note accurately. It would, therefore, be idle to expect a lay listener to be able to distinguish between such fine variations even when produced. They should consider themselves proud even with a definite recognition between a sharp and a flat variety of a note. In common practice the ordinary artists do not use the ideal scale of twenty-two *Shrutis* nor do the musical text-books refer to it. So, for all practical purposes, we should take the scale as consisting of twelve notes only; and I do so.

Musical Gharanas

As in literature, so in music, there are various schools of thought
called *Gharanas.* Literally, *Gharana* means a family. Even though
in actual life people may belong to the same caste, follow the same
religion and subscribe to the same creed, the families amongst them
differ in their traits, culture, ideology and the like. In music,
too, even when the same system is followed, the same *Raga* or the
same *Cheeza* (song) is sung or played, the style of the exposition
of that *Raga* differs with each *Gharana.* Why, the style is bound to
differ with every artist even though he may belong to the same
school of thought — the *Gharana.* But every artist cannot establish
a *Gharana* of his own. In order to constitute a *Gharana,* it must
have an ideology and merits powerful and outstanding enough to
establish an independent ' cult ' — sufficient to attract a band of
disciples and a host of admirers. So also a *Gharana* must have some
marked and peculiar features of its own to give it an individual
and distinct character.

Some *Gharanas* are known by their regional names such as
Gwalior Gharana, Agra Gharana; as the artists who were responsible
for the *Gayaki* (the style of singing) of that particular school belonged
to that region. Some *Gharanas* are known by the name of their
founder-artist, such as *Alladiyakhan Gharana* and *Abdulkarimkhan
Gharana.* The original founders gave an inspired exposition of their
art and at the same time preserved it by imparting *Vidya* (knowledge)
to their *Shishyas* (disciples). The disciples in turn did the same thing,
thus establishing a long succession of the teacher and the taught
to continue the tradition and the special features of their school or
Gharana. During the course of time, however, many a reputed
Gharana has become extinct; yet a few survive up to this date, and
they have their own exponents and admirers.

The *Gharanas* have, no doubt, survived; but not so the ideology
and distinctive qualities which they stood for. Whatever lofty
ideals and outstanding qualities a *Gharana* had when it came to be
established, the followers thereof could not maintain the high
level intact. They imitated the defects rather than the merits. As
a result, the position of many illustrious *Gharanas* at present
is miserable. In some, only the form appears to have been meticulously maintained but not the spirit underlying it. In others,
emphasis is being laid on the minor and weak points than on the

major and strong ones. In short, the present exponents of some of the *Gharanas* have nothing more to boast of than the illustrious name of their founder-*Guru* and the glorious past of the *Gharana*.

So, without referring to any particular *Gharana* (which may be unpalatable and controversial too) I would make some general observations as to why these *Gharanas* differ. I think they differ mainly on account of three factors : (1) emphasis on values, (2) method of presentation, and (3) choice of forms. For example, some give utmost importance to *Swara*, i.e., trying to make the note most melodious, powerful and appealing. This they would even do at the cost of other values in music. Some others, on the contrary, would place utmost emphasis on rhythm. That is, they would take pleasure in exhibiting a constant *Tala* consciousness throughout their performance, with the result that their *Alap*-making becomes rigid in design and stern in character. Some are conservative in their outlook. They would not like to transgress beyond the trodden paths of music. Thus, they would meticulously try to preserve the *Bandish* (composition) of their *Cheeza* (song), the set form of their *Ragas* and its improvisation too intact even when much of it requires change and improvement. Few others, on the contrary, have revolutionary tendencies. They would take pleasure in deviating from the accepted order. Thus, they would, by not observing the *Raga* rules, give rise to new *Ragas*, and would compose new *Cheezas* of their own to suit the new melodies. Some would concern themselves only with the scientific aspect, while others with the lighter aspect only. As a result, some earned reputation for their *Dhrupada* or *Khayal* while others for their *Thumri* or *Tappa*.

In method of presentation also, there appears a great divergence. Some would follow a ' point by point ' development method. That means, they would linger on very minute details to the extent that the whole picture or structure is seldom before the listener and his patience is tried. Others, on the contrary, would follow the ' bold brush ' method, that is, painting the whole picture by a very few strokes of the brush, caring only for the ' general effect '. The obvious defect of this system is that many a beautiful point and the pleasure which could have been derived from exploring the ' possibilities ' of the melody are denied to the listeners.

Some schools would lay stress on *Alap*, others on *Tanabazi* and still others on *Bol* or *Bol-Tana*. There too, in matters of detail, marked differences are apparent. Some would develop the *Alap* in a ' straight line ' fashion; while others would advance by ' curves '. In *Tanabazi*, too, we have some *Sapat* (flat) and simple designs and some *Gamak* and intricate patterns. Even *Raga* rules differ with the *Gharanas*. For example, in *Deshi*, some use *Shuddha* Dha, some *Komal* Dha, while others use both the variations.

A word of caution which I want to sound rather loud here is that the listener should not be the partisan of any particular school, as the fans and followers of the particular school are. Such an attitude is unhealthy, inasmuch as it makes one blind to the merits of others, as well as to one's own defects. An ideal *Gharana* like an ideal individual, is yet to be born. Please note that mere addition of good qualities does not necessarily produce a good piece of art. Art is not a machine-product but an individual creation. Admixture of merits and demerits, as well as differences, are bound to be there. It is this admixture and differences which give them an individual character and that is why our attraction for them is greater. So let us take things as they are. The different *Gharanas* are like different flowers. Each flower has its own fragrance and excellence. A person may have a liking or fascination for some particular varieties, but that is no good reason why he should condemn the others. As a real connoisseur of music, one must try to understand and appreciate a piece on its own merits and for no other extraneous consideration. Thereby many a point of excellence would unfold itself to the listener which would otherwise have been hidden or lost.[4]

Music and Rasa

In the preceding pages, I have made several references, such as, ' the moods ' of the *Ragas*, the ' emotional appeal ' of scientific and light music and the *Rasa Siddhi* in classical music. It is desirable, therefore, that I should try to explain the meaning and import of these words to the average listener in simple terms.

The first appeal of music is obviously to the sense of hearing

---

[4] Here is one more subject of which no apt demonstration can be possibly given. The teacher, at most, can exhibit the style of his own *Gharana*. In most cases, a student of music does not receive a comparative training in other styles besides the main style of his choice. The teacher should, therefore, try to explain only the broad distinction amongst the different styles on the lines indicated by me.

— to the ear — and through it music of whatever kind, gives at least a sensuous pleasure. But music cannot be classed as an art if it ends with making a sensuous appeal or giving a sensuous pleasure alone. The appeal of musical art, as of all other arts, must be an emotional one, i.e., an appeal to the feelings such as joy, sorrow, love, anger and so on. Such an appeal gives a vision of beauty which ultimately results in yielding aesthetic pleasure, certainly deeper and different in character from mere sensuous pleasure. That is why, it is said, that the chief purpose of all art is to give an aesthetic pleasure. The essential quality in Indian music, which is responsible for creating an emotional appeal and for giving an aesthetic pleasure may be called the *Rasa*, the ' life-juice ' or 'content' of Indian music.

Further questions arise as to what factors are responsible for producing this *Rasa*; and what is the nature of the *Rasa* thus produced.

The main factors that go to complete a musical performance can be enumerated as follows: (1) the note, (2) the rhythm, (3) the pattern or design, (4) the musical form, (5) the poetical content, (6) the *Raga*, (7) the presentation, and (8) the artist. That the combination of all these factors would produce the *Rasa* is an obvious answer. That note, the rhythm and the artist, without whose presence music is impossible, are indispensable factors, is a statement which cannot also be disputed. The real question is which of these is the most important factor that goes to produce the *Rasa*.

According to the ancient writers the note first and then necessarily the *Raga*, are the main factors which are responsible for producing *Rasa*. To each individual note, why, even to a *Shruti*, they have ascribed a specific inner meaning or emotive value. They have given different names — thereby suggesting different emotive values — to each of the twenty-two *Shrutis*. That a particular *Shruti* or *Swara* is capable of producing a particular fixed emotion is rather too difficult to accept. It must be admitted that the *Swara* must have an element of *Rasa*. But this means nothing more than to say that an individual note has a capacity to delight. If, on the other hand, a fixed emotive value to a note is ascribed then necessarily it shall have to be accepted that a *Raga* which is a combination of several notes would produce a mixture of several (perhaps diverse in their character) moods. This would certainly conflict with the accepted position that *Raga* produces a particular *Rasa* or mood. Then it is said that a *Raga* has also a particular *fixed* emotional appeal. An attempt to interpret the *Rasa* theory of music in terms of the *Nava Rasa*[5] theory of the *Sanskrit Natya Shastra* (nine *Rasas* according to the science of Dramatics) is also made. Instances of *Ragas* like *Jogi, Asawari* and others are cited to establish that they have *Karuna* (pathos) as their *Rasa*.

While admitting that *Raga* has *Rasa* in the sense that it has an aesthetic appeal, it is difficult to accept, here also, that each *Raga* has a particular fixed emotion of its own, that is, one out of the *Nava Rasa*.

With regard to instances which are quoted such as *Asawari* for pathos, *Adana* for heroism, etc. it is true that we feel that certain *Ragas* do produce feelings of pathos, joy or vigour. But this can be explained on the ground of consonant and dissonant relations of predominant notes used in that *Raga*. From experience gained as a result of tests on sonant-consonant relationship we can safely say that a specific combination of notes produces a specific effect on the mind of the listener.[6] Thus it is found that the use of consonant notes makes the music bright, lively and gay; while the use of dissonant notes makes the music sad, dull and depressing. In other words, the appeal thus created can be broadly divided into two major human emotional reactions, viz., joy and sorrow. This is why a feeling is created that certain *Ragas* do produce certain emotions.

But here, too, it should be noted that in the case of such a combination of notes, the appeal of *Ragas* would be limited to two major feelings at the most and that too in the case of a small number of *Ragas* only. It is difficult to ascribe, in this fashion, any particular emotional appeal to a majority of *Ragas*. The old masters

[5] The following are the *Nava Rasa* according to *Sanskrit* rhetorics: *Shringar* (amorous or erotic), *Veer* (heroic), *Karuna* (pathos), *Adbhuta* (wonder), *Hasya* (mirth or humour), *Bhayanakara* (dreadful), *Beebhatsa* (disgust), *Roudra* (anger or furiousness) and *Shanta* (peace or tranquillity).

[6] For convenience, I give below a table showing the relation of each note to the tonic and the nature of consonance or dissonance it produces :

The Tonic and its octave	Absolute consonance
With Ma and Pa	Perfect consonance
With *Ga* Ga and Ni	Medial consonance
With Ri and Dha	Imperfect dissonance
With *Ri*, Má, *Dha, Ni*	Complete dissonance

themselves must have felt the difficulty, as they did not attempt, as in the case of a *Swara* or *Shruti*, to ascribe a particular emotion to a particular *Raga* — barring, of course, a few exceptions mentioned above.

While dealing with the topic of *Raga* and *Tala*, I said that each *Raga* has a different mood or colour. The use of the word ' mood ' or 'colour' was purposeful as thereby I did not want to import the idea of a particular fixed emotion. What I wanted to say was that each *Raga* has a character of its own and has, so to say, a different ' audible colour'.

Some say that it is the poetical content of the song that is mainly responsible for the *Rasa-Siddhi*. In two respects this statement appears to be correct. In music where words predominate, (vide Chapter IV), i.e., where emphasis is on words rather than on *Swara*, the words of the song may help to produce the emotion expressed in the musical piece. Another instance is provided by the ' occasional' music, i.e., sung for a particular purpose or occasion, such as Stage-music. Here, the music may serve to produce the effect appropriate to the occasion or situation; for the music is so composed and so presented. In this limited sense only, can the *Nava Rasa* theory be applied to musical *Rasa*-theory.

But barring these exceptions, it cannot be said that the poetical content of the song is mainly responsible for the *Rasa-Siddhi* in music. The main difficulty in the way of accepting this basis is that the emotional aspect of instrumental music — which is music without words — cannot then be possibly explained. Scientific music or ' *Swara*-predominating' music (for explanation see Chapter IV) where the words of the song or its poetical content have very little importance, would present another difficulty.

Like poetical content, the slow or fast tempo of the rhythm also helps to produce a particular mood. So is the case with certain forms of music which I have dealt with in the last chapter. What is to be noted here is that all these factors may *help to enhance* a particular mood or be conducive to creating that particular mood. But they are not primarily responsible for generating any such mood.

I think, the factor *primarily* and *mainly* responsible for establishing the *Rasa* is the artist himself. It is the artist's conception and his emotional interpretation which finds expression through any art. It is therefore he who has to infuse the ' life ', the emotional content, into music. The *Swara*, the *Laya*, the pattern, the *Raga*, etc., are, after all his media. These media, like water or white colour, partake of that colour which the artist chooses to mix them with. For this he may make such a selection of the media and the means which would be more useful and helpful. But the media and the means alone can never be decisive factors. Even with poor stuff, a master artist can produce amazing results. (That is why I have said earlier, that folk-music can attain the classical height.) On the contrary, an artist lacking in intuition, imagination and inspiration is bound to make a mess of all the good factors in music at his command. (That is why, much of scientific music suffers nowadays.) A song in *Jogi Raga* can also be sung in a way to create heroic atmosphere. On the contrary, a *Cheeza* in *Adana Raga* can be sung in a way to create a feeling of entreaty. So what matters most in *Rasa-Siddhi* is the emotional urge, the inspiration and the imagination of the artist and his method of presentation. All other factors do help or are more or less contributory; but are not self-sufficient.

But whatever that may be, when music attains the height of classical music, the *Rasa* kindled in such a case bears no comparison to any of the *Nava Rasas* of our Sanskrit Rhetorics. As said in an earlier chapter, the *Rasa* of classical music is quite free from ordinary feelings of joy, sorrow, etc. i.e., it has not got any utilitarian basis but possesses a sort of transcendental element in it. The aesthetic pleasure resulting from it is quite pure, unique and unrelated to any fulfilment of desire. The end and aim of all musical art must be the attainment of this real *Rasa-Siddhi*. In other words, the excellence in music will be judged by the standard it attains in *Rasa-Siddhi*.

The Mahafil (concert)

I do not think that the *Mahafil* proper of Indian music is correctly described by the word concert or even a chamber-music concert. The *Mahafil* presents before my eyes quite a different picture. First of all it is a small and compact gathering in a well-appointed drawing hall and not a huge congregation in a 'public place of entertainment'. The well-lighted hall with white sheetings spread all over the floor; covered, at places, with colourful carpets and comfortable *Takiyas* and *Lods* [7] filled with profuse scents and

---

[7] *Takiyas* and *Lods* — kinds of bolsters for the convenience of reclining.

the aroma of smoke; and provided with a heavily loaded *Pandan* [8]—creates a luxurious and delightful atmosphere to begin with. There the chief artist is seated at a central place, with two *tambura* players close behind him, and with the *tabla* player on his right and a *sarangi* player on his left — both expert artists, ready to accompany and at times even to ' suggest ' or ' lead ' him. The audience seated on the same floor and level closely cluster round the artist in a crescent-like fashion, leaving no vacant corridor or space in between. The first ranks are filled by brother artists and staunch connoisseurs of music, i.e., by people who *justify* their proximity on the strength of their merits and not on the strength of their ' power ' or ' pocket '. And the eagerly waiting audience behind them — in short, the atmosphere is very lively, fervent and favourable for the great event to follow.

The peculiar seating arrangement, let me say, is not arbitrary or fanciful; but is necessary and thought out. As said above, the front ranks have to justify their position in two ways. They have to *respond*. Though the music starts with the modest idea of providing simple entertainment, it has — if it is music worth the name — soon to rise to a higher emotional level and to attain the *Rasa-Siddhi*, its ultimate goal. The selected audience close by must, therefore, help the artist to rise to that level. Such a response, then, cannot be a silent one, i.e., with the ears only; but it must be a visible and eloquent one manifested by the whole of the physical being dancing in harmony with the rhythm, so that the artist also knows that the audience is with him. Ultimately the aesthete so identifies himself with the artist that he sings — of course mentally — the song with the singer and beats with him the musical rhythm. No wonder, therefore, that stimulated by such an active response, the artist is doubly inspired, is completely drawn out and the audience gets the utmost that the artist is capable of creating.

These ' selected few ' in the front ranks owe also a duty to the bulk of the congregation behind them. These ' back-benchers ' are not endowed with the same capacity of understanding or appreciating the music, as the selected few are. Their enjoyment, appreciation and judgment of any performance, therefore, depends mostly on those of the ' inner circle '. So, if the interest of the latter is kindled, that of the whole congregation is also kindled. If the

[8] *Pandan* — A tray containing betel leaves, betel nuts and other material for chewing.

interest of the latter flags, that of the congregation also flags. In other words, these intermediaries — sitting as they do between the artist and the general audience — have to carry the message of music from the source to the entire congregation behind them.

This is of course a picture of an ideal *Mahafil* where not only is the seating arrangement ideal but the artists and the audience are also ideal. Such a coincidence is bound to be rare. The lot of the average listener is quite otherwise. His craving for music is now mostly satisfied by the radio or the gramophone record, where his ears only are pressed into service. The television, which is now spreading fast, would supply one more deficiency. But after all, it is a machine that a listener has to face and not a living soul. Without undermining in any way the tremendous advantages of the radio and other mechanized music, I want to assert that it cannot be compared with the *Mahafil* proper; just as the cinematographic show cannot be compared with a live dramatic performance.

The average listener has rare chances of hearing music in private groups — especially that of a master artist. The master artist has become, nowadays, both a rare and a dear commodity which is available only in the musical commercial markets [9] which are held in the form of gigantic concerts. It is regrettable that even music circles should sometimes assume the same form. Fortunately the number of concerts, on a limited scale or of private nature, though of second-class artists, is big enough, even now, to give an average listener an opportunity of listening directly and closely to a musical performance.

But whether a listener attends a big concert or a small gathering, there are certain canons of general behaviour which he should observe in order to maintain the atmosphere of the *Mahafil*. The rules which I am enumerating on the next page are not meant only for the lay listeners but for those 'selected few' of the 'inner circle' also, who many a time misuse their privilege and are guilty of violating them.

[9] Yes, commercial because such concerts are mostly arranged on the basis of money investments and their returns. That is why, artists are selected on their 'drawing value'. That is why, box collection programmes like *Jugalbandi* — which assume the form of a 'free style' fight between the artists — and ravishing dances are arranged. As a result, the artists do not put their heart in the performance; nor does the audience have any fervour or enthusiasm about it. All this is aggravated when musical 'party-politics' sometimes get the upper hand resulting in hooting out an artist the stage before he has finished.

(1) When music is going on, chit-chatting and laughing should be avoided. It is not a radio programme you are listening to, which does not enjoin any restriction on your behaviour.

(2) Do not enter the hall — as many take pride in so doing — so as to distract the attention of the artist or the congregation. To leave the hall in the middle is still more deprecable.

(3) The artist may be your favourite; but even then, do not overdo your part while giving applauses and responses. In the reverse case, do not openly show your disapproval, nor keep mum and throw cold water on the artist's enthusiasm. Others, who may be depending on your judgment, may unnecessarily form a wrong opinion about the artist.

(4) As regards *Farmaish* (suggestion) you cannot be too discreet. First of all, remember that sending a letter to the Radio Station as regards your *Farmaish* is not the same thing as making a suggestion to an artist in a *Mahafil*. The golden rule is not to make any suggestion at all. Better leave the artist to make his own choice. Unless you know his repertoire, i.e., you know what he knows, in what he excels and unless you know what befits the occasion, you may not make a suggestion.

Without going further, I may sum up: do not treat the artist as a mere caterer of music even if you have paid for it and do not think that you are there merely for merry-making. Through music you are to achieve something higher — self-oblivion and self-elevation.

But it would be doing injustice to listeners to suggest that it is they alone who are responsible for disturbing the atmosphere and harmony of the *Mahafil*. The artist is also responsible for it. At times, it is he who starts the trouble. It would not, therefore, be out of place if I point out the canons which the artist is also supposed to observe :

(1) The artist should, first of all, be well in time at the place of performance. This applies to accompanying artists also.

(2) He should be particular about the choice of his accompanying artists and their instruments *before hand*.

(3) Avoid meticulous tuning of the instruments in the presence of the audience.

(4) Even first-class artists should not spend more than half an hour for the first *Khayal*. Nine out of ten who take more time than

this do nothing better than repeating and tiring out the patience of the audience. For further pieces also a judicious use of time should be made. Please note that it is the quality that matters and not the quantity.

(5) Do not attempt to sing the *Ragas* or forms of music over which you have no mastery. What matters is not how much you know but what best you know; and again, not what you sing but how you sing.

(6) Along with the intrinsic culture of your music, the flourishes of hand, the facial expression and other mannerisms of yours must also bear testimony to your general culture.

(7) Whatever you sing, see that you are taking the audience with you. Do not rejoice very much in the fact that the audience has not understood you at all.

(8) The accompanists should bear in mind that they are there to help and not to hinder the main artist.

It is no use adding to this list. The success of a *Mahafil* depends upon the cooperative efforts of all concerned. So, if you want to have an ideal *Mahafil*, the musician, the music, the accompanists, the seating arrangement, the atmosphere and the listeners — all must be ideal.

Music and Nature

For other arts like painting and sculpture, Nature provides a fund of images and models from which the artist can freely draw or imitate. To music, however, Nature lends nothing of this sort. Sounds and rhythm, the chief constituents of music are undoubtedly found in Nature. But such sounds which are heard in Nature hardly bear any comparison to the sweetness of the trained human voice or to the sweetness of the sound which the musical instruments produce, let alone the musical scale and the very developed and intricate musical creation. In literature, we do find references to the utterances of the cuckoo or the nightingale as musical; but it has only a relative elementary significance as compared with the highly evolved and trained human voice. Perhaps it is ' sweet ' only as a contrast to the utterly coarse and harsh cries of other animals and birds.[10]

[10] Some old text-writers have gone to the length of comparing each note of

M 6

My point is that apart from the fact that the rudiments of music are found in Nature, the developed music that we have today is essentially a human creation. Man has gone on imitating and improving all by himself. The student of music, therefore, has to learn by actually imitating another. That accounts for the long succession or chain of the Teacher and the Taught (*Guru Shishya Parampara*) in vogue in our music. The task of the mere listener is still difficult. As he is not going to imitate, he has to memorize and when he listens again he has to bring before his mind the audible images in order to compare and contrast. This may appear rather difficult; but it is not so. Your ears when trained a little can do it as mine or any one else's can do.

Music and Miracle

Whether due to mythological influences or otherwise our idea of greatness of anything is always associated with something unknown, wonderful and miraculous. Well, music is no exception to this. So, whatever I might have said about the great things in music, the discussion would not be complete unless I say something about its mystical and miraculous aspects also.

Thus, one must have heard about the *Raga Megh-Malhar*, the powerful *Tanas* of which can bring about a storm followed by torrential showers of rain; about the *Deep Raga*, the luminous *Alaps* of which can make the candles or lamps ablaze and about the strong appeal of music which not only can melt human hearts but the hardest of stones, the diamond. Though I have heard and read about such anecdotes and also witnessed some such effects on the Screen, I cannot persuade myself to treat them on any higher level than pure myths or legends or the imaginative and metaphorical rendering of psychological and emotional effects on the human mind. I wish that the listeners should not indulge in such beliefs. But to those who would not be dislodged from their faith in such stories and would vouch for their truth on the basis of their accounts in old books, I may only say that our generation is very unlucky

the musical scale with the utterance of some bird or animal. Thus *Shadja* is sounded by the peacock, the goat bleats *Gandhara*, *Dhaivat* is the neigh of the horse or is croaked by a frog, *Nishad* is trumpeted by the elephant and so forth. The only thing I can say about this is that gone are the good old days when such animals and birds were so musically gifted !

in not having such great masters and such great music !

The influence of music on animals and other living beings and organisms is not, however, a matter shrouded in mystery as the above, but is a matter about which we often hear in the present times. Thus we need not go to the mythological days of Lord Krishna who by means of his *murali* (flute) charmed the *gopies* and cows alike. Stories or reports of snakes being charmed by the *pungi* (a flute-type instrument) of the snake-charmer, of dogs listening to music and producing some notes even, of buffaloes yielding more milk when listening to music, of fields giving bumper crops when surcharged with music, and of diseases being cured by music, are heard and read by us even today. It is not easy to ignore or doubt these accounts as many of them are reported to be the results of scientific research. I am more concerned, however, with the effects which music can produce on human beings. I realize, with much pain, that most good music does not have the salutary effect which it should have on the majority of people. I, therefore, sincerely wish that the experiments referred to above should come out successful so that the human being should learn a lesson from other living beings and organisms and should not at least lag behind them in musical appreciation.

7. METHODS OF EDUCATION

So far I have discussed a number of aspects of Indian music, viz., its constituents, values, forms, classification and miscellaneous problems arising out of it. The subject can be further developed. However, the treatment given so far is, I consider, sufficient for the average listener to get an idea as to what are the ideology and the special features of music, and to be able to distinguish broadly between what is high and low or good and bad in music.

But I am conscious that, after all, what I have stated is of an introductory nature and is not sufficient by itself to take any average listener into the real 'core' or 'sanctuary' of musical art. I wonder whether a few more books on the subject giving a detailed analysis, or voluminous descriptions of the minute intricacies of the science and art of music will enable one to achieve that result. It is the listener who must help himself to reach the 'sanctuary'. The aim of this book is, first to create in the listener a desire to move, then to show him the way and also to help him a little when moving. Another object of the book is to remove the many preconceived notions and probable misconceptions about music and persuade the listener to give a serious consideration to the art of music. If I have awakened any such desire, helped his ears to discriminate between the right and the wrong, corrected some of his misconceptions and shown him the right perspective, I shall feel the satisfaction of having achieved a good deal.

From the point of view of serious students of music (also of staunch connoisseurs and artists) I have not said much in the sense that I have not entered into the intricacies of musical science or into the details of actual rendering of musical art. They would thus find many things said here elementary or of an introductory nature. While admitting this to be so, I want to point out further that along with basic facts this book makes a humble attempt to give also some basic principles, some perspective and some glimpses into the ultimate ideology of the science and art of music. The student should note that without understanding the basic principles correctly or without having a true perspective of the education

he is receiving, no length of time, no amount of learning, no labour
would get him to the desired level. If this book, therefore, is of
some use from this point of view, I shall feel that my labour is
rewarded.

The Teacher I want

I have said times without number, that all the discussion in this
book should be demonstrated by a music teacher. It is better
that I say what sort of a teacher I have in mind.

Music teachers or artists-*cum*-teachers are nowadays quite
numerous. But knowing rather well their standard I do not think
that they would be of much use for the peculiar job they are expected
to do. Unfortunately, the training which a music teacher ordinarily
receives is very scanty and lop-sided from many points of view.
He generally knows one class of music (either scientific or light).
There, too, he is not very well acquainted with all its forms. About
voice-culture or ornamentation, seldom is he aware of its comparative merits and defects. Most of our listeners are not probably
endowed with *Swara-Dnyana*. To get *Raga Sangeet* across to a
person who has no knowledge of *Swara-Dnyana* is really a difficult
job, because the listener is not going to imitate as disciples of music
do. He would simply listen. A teacher therefore must be an all-
rounder. He must be fairly acquainted with various kinds and
forms of music. He must be acquainted with *Gharanas* other than
his own. Besides, he must be able to answer the ' whys ' and ' why
nots ' in music. Above all, he must be able to *demonstrate effec-
tively* at a moment's notice whatever he knows. In other words he
must be an artist plus an educator.

Such an artist-*cum*-teacher to come up to our standard and
expectation has to be specially trained. In other spheres of education,
modern educational theory considers it necessary to educate the
teacher in the art of teaching, in addition to his possessing knowledge of his subjects. Similarly, our teacher will have to be specially
trained through an institution specially established for that purpose.
A course for such training will have to be formulated ; and other
details shall have to be worked out.

Special Courses in Appreciation

Now let me suggest as to how and where the experimental courses in musical appreciation can be tried. Nothing less than a regular course would be necessary. The following would be the main features of the course :

(1) About forty lessons (each of one hour's duration) would be adequate to complete a full course for training the uninitiated. For those whose general background of music is prepared and whose general understanding is also advanced, the number of lessons may be reduced to a half.

(2) The strength of the class should not be unwieldy. The teacher is expected to pay personal attention to the students and take various tests.

(3) Selected gramophone records, tape-recorded performances and suitable current radio programmes should be pressed into service. If possible, artists and experts should be requested to give demonstrations once a week. All such demonstrations should be preceded and followed by suitable introduction and commentary.

(4) Questions and answers and tests of various kinds should be a regular feature.[1]

Music Circles

Music Circles can do certain solid work in this direction. We may be justified in expecting this work from them. It is true that a member of a Music Circle is not as backward in musical appreciation as a layman is. But it must also be admitted that he is not as advanced as a real connoisseur of music is. These 'back-benchers', as I have said before, have to depend upon the 'selected few' of the 'inner circle' for their appreciation and enjoyment of a programme. The organizers of the Music Circles should not, therefore, remain contented, as they now are, with merely arranging different types of musical programmes. Side by side, attempts to train the ears of their members by other methods should be made. They can arrange some demonstrative lectures for the

[1] The author has himself tried such experiments and whatever has been written above is based on his personal experience.

purpose where members can exchange ideas and elicit information by asking questions. At the time of their regular programmes, introductory remarks, if possible some short explanatory commentary, at least some necessary information of the *Raga* and *Tala* and other details of pieces sung can be advantageously given. Music Circles are the places for fostering the right type of appreciation of the art of music ; for its members are equipped with the necessary grounding in music.

All India Radio

The All India Radio can do very much in this direction. Their facilities and resources are great. Music takes the lion's share of their ' time ' and ' money ' budget. The voice of the Radio has reached the rural ear too. To spread genuine Indian music and to create a taste for such music appears to be their aim. In fact, the institution has certainly a number of activities and facilities to implement its laudable aim.

No direct attempts, however, to educate the average listener as to how to appreciate music are being made.[2] To broadcast actual musical programmes of various kinds and allow the listener to develop his taste for it, is, in a sense, an *indirect* method, or at least a slow method. The Radio gives him only the ' finished product '. The listener must also be acquainted with the ' raw material ', the ' workshop process ' or the ' inner working ' of it. What I mean by this will be quite evident from whatever I have written before and hence without going into details I may just make a few broad suggestions here :

(1) A complete series of demonstrative talks in appreciation of music on the lines discussed in this book or in any other better way, can be arranged. The series may, then, be repeated like the series of ' Lessons in Hindi '.

(2) A few familiar *Ragas* and their oft-quoted *Cheezas* should be constantly repeated with a view to acquaint the listener with those *Ragas*. Some weeks (say like a ' Bhairav Week ' ' Miya-Malhar Week ') could be celebrated with this view.

[2] Some programmes under the head of ' Appreciation of Music ' are being arranged on the A.I.R. But the programmes contain much material useful only to a student of music. The uninitiated average listener is not kept in view.

(3) *Gayaki* of different *Gharanas,* so also different styles in *Thumri,* etc., could be suitably exhibited.

(4) After a master-artist's *Cheeza* is over and before he begins his next, a short commentary pointing out the highlights of his performance could sometimes be arranged.

In the foregoing chapters, enough suggestive material can be found and the All India Radio with its tremendous resources in men and means can do useful service along these lines.

Appeal to the Film-producers

The Music Circles, the All India Radio, the educational institutions and the like cannot deny, in principle, the thesis that education, with a view to cultivating taste for good music, must be given in some form or the other. To such institutions, one can make suggestions, with force, as to how they should move in that direction. But the position of the Film industry is quite different. They make use of music, and profusely too, but for their *own ends only.* One of these ends appears to be the intensification of the tempo of a scene or situation. Here the film producers have many problems of their own. For instance, they have to depict the caprices of nature, and the experiences of the hungry, the infirm, the insane, the oppressed, the destitute and the like. The music which is to serve such situations and heighten their effect must be necessarily of a different type. It is better that this ' *music* of exigency ' is left out of consideration.

But the Film provides music for another and equally important purpose, viz., pure entertainment. In respect of such music I am tempted to make an ' appeal ' to the Producers and Directors concerned.

Here, too, I know there are many handicaps. The business point of view, the limitations of the machine, the very short time at one's disposal and above all, the poor capacity of the masses to understand good music, are factors which cannot be ignored. Circumscribed by these limitations, the film-music must necessarily be of a different type. I must admit that the full-fledged *Raga Sangeet,* the music that dilates on extensive elaboration and improvisation or, in other words, the music which is difficult to understand and to follow is not suitable. Attempts to introduce difficult *Raga*

Sangeet were done in the early days of the sound-pictures ; but they have failed. Nor can the Stage-music be deemed the ideal. Even the Stage suffered on account of the music that flourished there. So, music which is simple in character but very attractive in design, and music which is ' catchy ' must be employed. Why, such music has been employed on the screen, and very successfully too.

But what is objectionable is the ' out-of-the-way experiments ' in producing cheap and hybrid varieties under the specious name of harmonization which have not only proved detrimental to our musical system but have degenerated the taste of the masses. Some justify this under the ' demand and supply ' principle. First of all, I very much doubt whether our cine-goers ever made such a demand. I am afraid that this sort of creation must be rather the outcome of the extreme fascination which the Directors themselves felt for Western music and of their inordinate desire to supply something novel. And even supposing that there is a popular demand for such varieties, should we cater for it ? Should we not mould and cultivate their taste if it is degenerating?

On the contrary, it appears that the cine-goers have cherished the *Raga Sangeet*, and good light varieties very much. Such songs still linger in their ears even though the pictures which featured them have been long forgotten.[3]

My plea is, therefore, very simple. In every Film let there be at least *two* songs which would conform to some good forms of Indian music, whether *Raga Sangeet* or music of the ' light licentious ' type does not so much matter. Let it remind the listener of some good melody of some good form of *our* music. Even with this, balance of about six other songs would remain for all other purposes and other experiments. I hope my suggestion would find favour as a practical one too.

If this simple thing is done, much ground, from the point of view of musical appreciation, would be gained. The ' voice ' of the Screen practically reaches all the ' ears ' and it has a special fascination for the ' young ears '. The Stage-music which once did very good service in cultivating the taste for good music is

[3] Take for instance the Hindi songs like ' Zindaki Usi Ki Hai ', ' Jadugar Saiya ', ' Nain Se Nain ', ' Leke Pahala Pahala Pyar ', ' Sari Sari Raat Teri ', ' Muze Na Bulao ', ' Ehasan Tera ', ' Madhubaname Radhika ', Gaye to Gaya Kaha, and Marathi songs like 'Maza Hoshil Ka', 'Thakalere Nandalala', ' Kabraiche Shele Vinato ' and ' Vajavi Murali Sham '.

fast declining — and the Screen is indirectly responsible for it. So let me appeal to all those concerned in the Film industry to give a serious consideration to the problem and thus serve the cause of music.[4]

What about the Artist?

A question is often asked whether the artist himself does anything special to cultivate the average listener's taste for music. First of all, it is not proper to expect the artist to do this. The functions of the Artist and those of the Commentator are quite distinct ; and it is not even desirable that the Artist should be the Commentator too !

The artist, nevertheless, must be able to appreciate his own art. What I mean is, that he must develop the healthy habit of holding the ' mirror of introspection ' before his eyes. (Even an ordinary mirror would be a good corrective for too many gesticulations !) Such a ' mirror ' would reveal so many things : his merits and demerits, his vain pride for the *Gharana* or the *Guru*, disproportionate and parasitic developments in his *Gayaki*, his maddening haste, his craze for novelty, his contentment regarding the grammatical and the mathematical aspects of the music, and so many other things. Such a ' mirror ' would help him to see himself as others see him. Self-introspection is perhaps the best corrective. Even if it is too late for correction or well nigh impossible, such a mirror would, at least, help one to know where he stands — and that is no mean achievement. It would be noted that if the average listener does not feel attracted by music that is good, it is not only his ignorance that is responsible. The disregard of the artist himself about the proper perspective and the true goal of the art and the consequent defective performance are also responsible for it.

So if the artist sees for himself what is good and what is bad and presents his art more thoughtfully, I think, the task of education in musical appreciation would be made very easy.[5]

---

[4] Some suggest that it is up to the Film Censor Board to put a check on the unwholesome tendencies in the musical production of the sound pictures. I doubt whether the Board by itself can remedy the evil. I do not, at the same time, desire that in matters of artistic and cultural taste, restrictions and regimentation should play any part.

[5] My remarks are with regard to *artists* only. Formerly the ' artist ' was also

Government and Educational Institutions

The real forum of the education of musical appreciation is the Government and the educational institutions. For it is in the educational institutions where *every* citizen of tomorrow is bound to spend a few years of the very best part of his life. It is here that systematic courses can be arranged and methodical education can be imparted.

In most of the primary schools, I believe, very simple music (at least recitation of poetry set to some tunes), is taught. Those are the most favourable years for training in intonation also. In the secondary schools, however, music is an optional art-subject and very few students avail of the education. Some universities have included music as a subject for degree courses even.

But all this arrangement is for those who wish to choose music as their optional subject, and want to learn music. But what about the majority of students who do not want to learn music for one reason or the other? Should they not know something of this art as they do in the case of appreciation of poetry, drama, etc. in their usual course of studies? In the case of music, the necessity for such an education is great ; for music is of the very essence of human life and is, besides, one of the greatest cultural heritages with which every citizen of this country must be acquainted. But, unfortunately, this cultural education is being neglected.

I have not a first-hand knowledge of what is being done in the Western countries in this respect. It appears that the Soviet Union gives great importance to the study of such cultural subjects. I am giving below an extract from one of the letters sent by Shri J. P. Naik, the famous educationist (at present the Adviser for Primary Education, Government of India) when he was touring in Russia on an educational mission :

> Here all recreation is State controlled. All actors and actresses, all the ballerinas, etc., are State servants. And it is the ballerinas that receive the highest salary in Russia — far much more than what even the Ministers receive. . . . I find that the average

the ' teacher '. But with the spread of musical education the ' teacher ' has been separated from the ' artist '. So here when I use the word ' artist ' I do not want to refer to the present-day vast majority of persons who are merely music teachers.

Russian is very greatly interested in music, drama and dance. In all the schools that we visit, we find a great emphasis on these activities and particularly on music. Hence in teacher-training institutions also, there is a great emphasis on music, dance and drama. We saw a teacher-training institution where music was a compulsory subject and it was studied for five years. As education is widespread and compulsory the children imbibe the love of these fine arts very early. These attitudes are carried over in adult life and hence we find the public greatly devoted to the classical forms of all these arts. As the profession is State controlled, there is no falling down in standards, and expense is no consideration. In every town and even in rural areas there are several theatres. In Russia, education is interpreted to include, besides formal instruction in schools, the informal education through dance, drama and music.

I have quoted the letter at some length for it touches two vital points, from the point of view of our inquiry, viz., that the love of fine arts must be imbibed by the children from the very beginning and that education should compulsorily cover also the cultural subjects like dance, drama and music.

Whether it is possible to include the teaching of such subjects as compulsory ones is for the Education Department to consider. My expectation, in this matter, is very modest. I do not insist, let me repeat, on any *actual* education in music. Such education would be, in many cases, impracticable too. Many students, especially males, do not possess the necessary aptitude or even the suitable voice. What I want is education in *musical appreciation only*. The student has not to learn but simply to listen, and would get his education through a sort of entertainment, as one gets physical exercise through play. For such an education, no question of any barrier of age or aptitude, on the one side, and the budget and the educational establishment on the other, would come in. One period in a week would suffice and this instruction can be carried even to the College level of education. Nay, it should, by all means be carried to that stage ; for, the more mature the understanding is, the easier it is to grasp the aesthetic pleasures of art.

I know that there would be many practical difficulties in the way of implementing this idea. First of all, if the musical education is to be spread on a wider scale, sufficient number of music teachers may not be available. Again it would be difficult to get good music teachers for the rural areas. Another practical difficulty is that there are no means to judge the standards and capacity of the music teachers that are available. They may produce certain diplomas ; but in many cases, their ability would be only evident in their diplomas and not in their actual performances.

But some ways can be found out and I propose to make the following suggestions :

(1) A complete course of musical appreciation should be *tape-recorded* ; so that it can be exhibited by suitable instalments. The tape-reels and also the tape-recorder must be made available to the educational institutions at a very low price. A tape-recorder may thus serve as a substitute for the teacher.

(2) Another way to achieve the same result is to get a set of gramophone records prepared on the lines of Lingua-phones. Such a set also must be made available at a low price. These gramophone records would be useful where supply of tape-recorders is not practicable on account of want of electricity or otherwise.

(3) A Music Teacher's Training Centre or Institution should be established. This institution would specially coach the music teachers to be fit enough to impart the peculiar lessons in musical appreciation. Through such an institution the work of preparing tape-records and gramophone records, as suggested above, can be done and research for finding new methods and means can be undertaken.

It is no use adding to the list ; for one cannot be too sure of their success as such an experiment has never been tried before. We have to go, therefore, by ' trial and error method '. What I want to impress is that the Government and the educational institutions have to give an anxious consideration to the problem and have to make a beginning.

One of the aims of education is to give cultural orientation to the human mind. The study of art makes such orientation possible. Is it not, therefore, the duty of the Government and of educationists to create in the minds of the citizens of tomorrow a taste for genuine musical art which is one of the greatest components of our cultural heritage?

GLOSSARY

All Indian terms are shown in italics in the body of the book and are explained when they first occur. Meanings of some of the frequently used musical terms are given here. The peculiarity of pronunciation of certain vowels is shown in the words given in brackets below. Phonetic variations of the same vowel are shown by a dash above, but for the convenience of printing, the diacritical marks have been omitted in the text.

a (above ; or more appropriately as ' u ' in ' urge ';)
ā (far) ; i (sit) ; ī (as 'ee' in ' meet ') ; o (mode) ; u (bull)

AAS	Steadiness of note ; resilience of notes.
ABHIJĀT	Classical
ALANKĀRA	Ornament or embellishment
ALĀP	Slow movement exposition of *Raga* theme
ALĀPĪ	*Alap*-making
ANTRĀ	Second part of a *Cheeza*
ĀROHA	Ascending order of notes
ASTHĀĪ	First part of a *Cheeza*
AWAROHA	Descending order of notes
BHAJAN	A devotional song
BHĀV-GEET	A lyric song in Marathi language ; a form of light music
BOL	Words ; syllabic words used for vocalizing
BOLTĀNA	A *Tana* with words.
CHEEZA	A specimen composition characterizing a *Raga*
DĀDRĀ	A kind of *Tala* (Duple compound or 6/8 time) ; a musical form of light variety
DHAMĀR	A musical form of serious type sung in *Tala* of the same name
DHRUPADA	A musical form of serious type
GAMAK	A kind of serious musical ornament produced by reiteration of two notes giving the effect of violent shake or trill
GĀYAKĪ	Style of singing
GAZAL	A musical form of light variety in Urdu language ; lyric song in Urdu
GEETA	A song
GHARĀNĀ	A school of thought in music
KALĀ	Art

KAN	A grace note
KAS	Intensity or volume
KHATKĀ	A kind of popular musical ornament (Compare with ' Turn ' in Western Music)
KHAYĀL	A musical form of the serious variety
KOMAL	Flat (note)
LĀWANI	Most popular form of Maharashtrian folk-music
LAYA	Rhythm
LOKA-GEETA	Folk-song
MADHYA SAPTAK	Middle octave
MAHAFIL	A chamber-music concert
MANDRA SAPTAK	Lower octave
MĀTRĀ	The time unit in *Tala* ; a musical beat
MEEND	Glide (compare ' Portamento ' in Western Music)
MUKHADĀ	(Face) Opening phrase of a lyric
MURKĪ	A kind of popular musical ornament (compare with ' Nota Cambiata ' in Western Music)
NOM-THOM	A style of *Alap*-making with peculiar nonsense words
RĀGA	A melodic law or order ; a melody-type based on a modal scale
RASA	Aesthetic content or emotional appeal in music
RASA SIDDHĪ	Attainment of *Rasa*
SAMA	The first beat of a *Tala* ; the ' arrival point ' of a *Tala*
SAMVĀDĪ	The concordant note next in importance to the predominant (*Vadi*) note in a *Raga*
SANGEET	Music
SAPTAK	Octave
SARGAM	Solmization
SHRUTI	A microtone ; small discernible intervals lesser than semitone
SWARA	A note
SWARA-DNYĀNA	Ability to recognize pitch or interval of notes
SWARA-SĀDHANĀ	Voice-culture
TĀLA	Time cycle containing one or more sub-time measures
TAMBURĀ	A four-stringed instrument used to provide the drone
TĀNA	A rapid succession of notes ; semiquaver figures
TAPPĀ	A musical form of light variety
TARĀNĀ	A musical form using peculiar nonsense words
TĀRA SAPTAK	Higher octave
THUMRĪ	A musical form of light variety
TĪWRA	Sharp (note)
VĀDĪ	The predominant note in a *Raga*

BIBLIOGRAPHY

CLEMENTS, E.: *Lectures on Indian Music*
CLEMENTS AND DEVAL: *Publications of the Philharmonic Society of Western India*
FOX-STRANGWAYS: *The Music of Hindustan*
POPLEY, REV. H.: *The Music of India*
BHATKHANDE, PUNDIT V. N.: *Hindustani Sangeet Paddhati*, Four Volumes (Marathi)
RANADE, PROF. G. H.: *Hindusthani Music*
TEMBE, G. S.: *Kalpana Sangeet* (Marathi)
GOSVAMI, O.: *The Story of Indian Music*
MUKHERJEE, D. P.: *The Music of India*
JONES, SIR WILLIAM: *Music and Musical Modes of the Hindus*
WILLARD, CAPTAIN: *A Treatise on the Music of Hindustan*

M 7

INDEX

INDEX

101